D1027388

HOW TO STAND UP FOR YOURSELF

HOW TO STAND UP FOR YOURSELF

by
Paul A. Hauck

THE WESTMINSTER PRESS
Philadelphia

Book Design by Dorothy Alden Smith

Published by The Westminster Press®
Philadelphia, Pennsylvania

PRINTED IN THE UNITED STATES OF AMERICA

9 8 7 6 5 4 3

Library of Congress Cataloging in Publication Data

Hauck, Paul A
  How to stand up for yourself.

  1. Assertiveness (Psychology)   I.   Title.
BF574.A85H38   158'.1   78–15066
ISBN 0–664–24223–5

This book is dedicated to those unhappy people who have seldom controlled life to obtain from it the satisfactions it is possible to yield, and to my friend from Zagreb.

Contents

Preface

After finishing my eighth book I felt certain I would take a rest from this slavish profession. I had written enough. I was ready to read books for a while rather than write them.

Hadn't I already said enough about the psychology of mental health in my paperback quartet on depression, anger, fear, and self-discipline? Hadn't I expressed myself sufficiently in my latest book, *Marriage Is a Loving Business,* to let the matter rest? But, here I am, compelled to pick up pad and pen and do my thing.

I know I have another book in me, an important one. It has to do with persons' taking control of their own lives, something which if not done leads to endless conflict, neurosis, and unhappiness. Worst of all, it leads to psychological slavery. I'm referring to that all-important skill which makes a mature person out of a vegetable: self-assertion. If you don't have the ability or willingness to stand up for your own beliefs, your life slips under the control of others.

Why is it so important to prevent that from happening? Because you will become an unhappy person as surely as you would if you never had a friend. Your mission in life is to live it so that you experience as little *needless* pain as possible and to fulfill your talents for all their worth. You will certainly suffer, even for long periods of time, as you struggle to learn and become all you can become. But such struggle is necessary for your growth. Later, when you have become skilled in business, cooking, socializing, tennis, or whatever, a degree of contentment will enter your life which you never knew when you were a frightened child in an adult body.

To reach your full growth and to enjoy your earthly existence as much as possible, it is essential that you take an active interest in yourself. You cannot let others determine the course of your life and expect peace of mind. Standing up for yourself is one of those powerful human acts which at one stroke can eliminate guilt, overcome fear, and make anger unnecessary. But it requires the most serious form of self-discipline.

In the following pages I hope to show how you avoid asserting yourself, what the psychological consequences are when this happens, and how to develop a quiet strength that makes others take notice of you without your having to raise your voice or make a fist.

HOW TO STAND UP FOR YOURSELF

1

Nice to a Fault

He came into my office with one of the most challenging assignments I had ever been given. Sitting down opposite me, he leaned forward intently and said: "I want you to make a new person out of me. I don't like myself. I never have. I don't like anything about me. I don't like the way I speak, the way I walk, and most of all I don't like how I act around people. I feel so inferior to them that I allow myself to be used. People can get almost anything out of me. I want to be liked so much I tolerate their joking with me, taking advantage of me, borrowing my money, asking for rides, and expecting me to give parties. But they just come, eat my food, and leave. I haven't enough courage to insist they help pay some of the expenses from time to time. I haven't courage to ask them to include me in their social life after they leave my apartment. I'm just a prize sap. I smile through every insult and abuse like I loved it and wanted more."

This fellow was a successful businessman. He had confidence and intelligence enough when it came to dealing with his several employees. However, when he tried to function at the social level he was nice to a fault.

He wanted me to train him out of that habit. When possible, I try to move along in therapy at a fast pace to bring maximum relief in the shortest time. With Bill this was not to be. His problems were so deeply ingrained I knew it was going to take months before we'd notice any differences in his personality.

Bill had been put down repeatedly by his parents when he was growing up. Not only did they criticize the boy harshly when he goofed up, as children will, but on those occasions when he did well they remained silent. The net result of this treatment left him feeling he was always inadequate, always wrong. Feelings of inferiority produced intense shyness. It was painful for him to look people in the face. On one occasion he asked: "Why do I do that? What do my feelings of inferiority have to do with not looking people squarely in the eyes?"

"I think you feel that if people can't look into your eyes, they can't see inside of you, Bill," I replied.

"But what in heaven's name did I think they'd see if they could look inside me?"

"Trash, evil, worthlessness."

He studied the answer a moment and then lowered his head onto his arms on the desk and could not speak while he tried to recover his composure.

Bill had his ups and downs over the next year but he was a great student. He began to make strides in becoming a human being instead of a garbage can. He went on a self-improvement program that would have made any therapist proud. First he joined the local athletic club and began to work out on weights. From a plump, pudgy fellow he began to tighten up and trim down in a most impressive manner. That did some interesting things to his walk and his stance. Back came his shoulders, his head lifted up, his stride was brisk and long instead of short and quick.

Once his body was in shape he decided to take up sports. First it was bicycling, then tennis, and finally skiing. I could hardly believe how he was barreling along, changing weekly right before my eyes.

His clothes took a decided turn for the snazzy. Prior to therapy he wore nondescript things. They had no style or shape, let alone color. After consulting fashion magazines, he slowly began to experiment with color and styles. As a newcomer to the fashion world he naturally threw together some pretty strange combinations. However, he was alert to feedback and soon learned what harmonized and what clashed. When he came in one day wearing a red turtleneck sweater and a chain medallion around his neck I sensed that some profound changes had taken place.

Even his voice began to change. It actually got deeper while the subtle whine he usually used gradually faded. It seemed indeed as though he was becoming a new person week by week, at least in outer appearance. However, he still had not learned how to assert himself with women. At dances he would find himself alone toward the end of the evening because he wasn't aggressive enough to commit a woman to a cup of coffee after the dance. After buying numerous rounds of drinks and thinking he was really making out, he found that some fellows with more experience would pop the question to his various dance partners and off they'd go one by one before the place closed up and poor Bill would suddenly find himself alone. Once again he was beginning to suffer from his lifelong prob-

lem: being nice to a fault. And that was the next problem I knew we'd have to deal with if we were going to
progress.

During the second year of therapy I saw him only
occasionally, sometimes only once a month. He knew
what he had to do, however, and with his characteristic
energy he applied himself vigorously and I saw the day
when he became a different person psychologically. He
was no longer a buffoon, a sucker who could be taken
advantage of by his so-called friends. He stood up to
them on several occasions and they soon learned that
Mr. Milquetoast was now commanding respect. He
didn't need their friendship any longer. They quickly
sensed that. And not needing their approval gave him
strength to stand up for himself at the risk of being
rejected. That was the clincher. Once they lost that
hold over him he was free. Everything fell into place
after that.

The day arrived when every one of Bill's initial complaints was changed. He liked his looks, his walk, his
talk, his clothes, and most of all himself. Always the
gentleman, he was kind to people who treated him with
dignity and respect but wasted no time with people
who wanted to use him. He could smell them out with
little difficulty.

Not every therapist has the good fortune to have such
an experience in his professional life. It is uplifting, for
the therapist sometimes wonders if he is being reasonable in what he expects of his clients. Bill helped me to
see again that hard work and guidance can bring about
profound personality changes. Later, when I was working with another client whom I had some doubt about,
I would say to myself, "If Bill could change, anybody

can." I would then press on with greater confidence.

Being too nice is a major fault. It is not healthy for you or for others.

IT CAN RUIN YOUR MARRIAGE

Few people argue with the idea that standing up for your rights on the job, in your neighborhood, school, church, or even on a bus is wrong. Unless you prevent others from pushing you around, it is cautioned, you will be asked to work late at the job, neighbors will borrow all your tools, and ruffians may annoy you on the bus. There is truth to these allegations.

Then why are we constantly being told that we must give in to our mates if we want our marriages to succeed? Be as loving and as giving as you can and your mate will love you forever, so the thinking goes.

Forget it. It's not usually true at all. Not that I have anything against being a decent, loving, and charitable person. Mature people care for others. A world without people who do kindnesses when you're in a spot is not worth living in. But along with all that talk about being your brother's keeper, allow someone else to be *your* brother too.

You're in your marriage because you expect to be happier as a husband or wife than you would be alone. That's a healthy motive and a selfish one too. If you don't recognize this fact, you'll often feel guilty over wanting or getting your way, especially if your spouse is frustrated because you're satisfied.

The happier each of you is, the more stable the marriage. If you allow yourself to become neglected at the expense of doing all manner of niceties for your mate, three things will happen. First, your mate will think everything is just wonderful and the marriage is proceeding nicely, while you will feel more and more abused because your needs and deep desires are being ignored. That will make you mighty unhappy if it continues. You may become disturbed, neurotic, begin to drink, and maybe hate yourself. Second, you'll hate your mate. And third, you'll hate the relationship.

Instead of letting your marriage become lopsided, accept the fact that you have rights too. Put pressure on your mate until you get enough satisfaction to feel *just reasonably content.* I call that the JRC. It is a critical stage in any relationship. Unless you feel just reasonably content most of the time, you will surely be unhappy and your marriage will be in danger. The point to remember, however, is that it is *your* responsibility to maintain the JRC. If you let your mate grab all the pleasures and force you to knuckle under, you're doing a great job of ruining a good relationship. Contrary to what is generally thought, you do not build a good marriage by chronically sacrificing yourself out of a sense of deep love. You spoil the one you indulge and make yourself miserable. No relationship can stay healthy for long under those conditions.

IT INTERFERES WITH YOUR CREATIVITY

One of the greatest drawbacks of being a nice guy is that you tend to agree too readily with the opinions of others. If you truly want to be a creative person, you will follow your own inclinations. You cannot create art, literature, or new ideas if you do not have the courage to be different. Almost every talented person has had to see his or her work through to completion against the criticism of others. This means that you will often say to the world, "You are wrong and I am right." Conceited as that may sound, it's what talented persons had better do if they want their talent to flourish.

In my own case I have observed a direct relationship between my maturing assertiveness and my creativity. At this writing I have published eight books, am writing two weekly newspaper columns, am offering five different seminars to my community, and have contributed my own theories to the field of psychology on phobias, love, marriage, moral retardation, and depression.

These have been stimulating and gratifying experiences. They have been surprising as well. I was aware that I was expressing new thoughts, but I had no feeling for how they were being received until other professionals began to mention me in their writings and to ask me to speak to their professional groups. It was then that I understood how this total output was impossible unless I was somehow comfortable with being different and tolerant of potential ridicule from my colleagues—in short, with standing up for my personal views.

What if Edison had listened to the many who laughed at his belief that he could light up the world with a light bulb? And what about Henry Ford? Those who scoffed at him, "Why don't you get a horse?" wound up later driving a Model T.

If you want to make your mark, don't listen to the defeatists. Instead, accept the encouragement of the hopeful, the optimistic, the people who dream. Rejecting a new idea is always safe. It's when you step into new territory that you expose yourself to ridicule and folly. That's why those who don't take risks can feel so smug about their views.

We all know that great advancements have been made by daring thinkers doing things in new ways. But what about everyday activities? Is it important in your life to dare to be different? You bet it is. Bill found that out when he decided to change his personality. At first many of his friends thought he was overdoing it when he sought help with that transformation. But for once in his life he didn't care what they thought. Had he shrugged his shoulders and smiled sheepishly and given in to group pressure, that would have been the end of this self-improvement program.

"But what makes me so right," you ask, "that I should insist on putting up red curtains instead of the beige ones my mother wants?" Good question. What makes you so right is that it is what you want. Why do you always assume the opinions of others are necessarily better than your own? You'll know how right you are only after you do things your way. That's how you develop talent. Don't let people talk you out of your ideas. Become a bit conceited. Insist fifty million Frenchmen can be wrong. Push for your design, your tune, your color, your choice of flavoring, your ideas, and see what happens. If nothing special occurs, you've lost nothing. But suppose you put something together that has never been done like that before and you like it. Don't you see what you've done? You've created something. Something new under the sun has come into being because you weren't afraid to displease others. You decided to give your inner urges free wing, and look what happened!

Let others talk you out of taking a chance and you're

letting them dominate you. They choose your house for you, pick your stocks, and arrange your furniture. They exercise their talents at your expense, reducing the opportunities to exercise *your* talents. So what if someone arranges your room, what of it? Well, consider the case of a girl who came home from her honeymoon, went into her bedroom and suddenly realized that her mother had rearranged the whole thing in her absence. At that moment, in an act of complete defeat, this nice girl who always gave in to others, finally had it. She went into a deep psychotic state (lost contact with the world) and had to be cared for like a child. She rolled herself into a ball and didn't speak again for years.

This is an extreme example, but it does illustrate what can happen to your abilities, talents, and growth if you repeatedly attempt to be a nice person. Like anything good, you can also be nice to a fault.

IT'S A SURE WAY TO SPOIL OTHERS

Do you know what happens when you don't use your legs? They waste away, slowly but surely. The day inevitably comes when you can't walk at all. This has frequently been observed in India's beggars who maim themselves to gain greater sympathy and thus more alms.

Your character is much the same. If someone indulges you all your life, you're certainly going to be unsure of yourself and afraid of practically everything strange. You would think the opposite were true, wouldn't you? Not so! Getting your way in almost every instance makes you so weak you can't stand life when it becomes frustrating. Mothers and fathers who are too good to their children are actually being unkind to them in the long run.

This is one of the best reasons I can think of for asserting yourself: the health of the one you love. What better way to show affection than by being willing to endure the rejection and hostility of someone whose love you value? Can't you see what a sacrifice that is? What a risk? If you truly care about a person, don't overdo the kindness bit.

Richard is a young man, an only child, the idol of two well-to-do parents who have lavished their money and love on him for years. His mother was particularly prone to spoil him and she knew it.

When the boy had a tough homework assignment she'd help him. Instead of making him work for his money, she gave him a weekly allowance. He didn't even have to make his bed. His father protested this spoiling but he was a passive fellow who didn't want to make waves. So he allowed his wife to indulge the boy year after year.

All went well until the son went off to college. He would run out of money from time to time and call home in a desperate state and plead for emergency funds. Well, what was a good parent to do but write out a check for one hundred dollars. And the crisis passed.

The young man was eventually graduated and soon married. Now new problems arose. His wife simply wasn't prepared for his dependency expectations and she wasn't about to baby him. She refused to lay out his clothes, draw his bath, or bring coffee to him in bed on Sunday mornings. That was a real shocker to Richard. He did not know how to deal with such total rejection and unfairness. In fact, instead of being on the receiving end, he now found that he was expected to go to the giving end. His wife believed it was his duty to support her, to open doors for her, to carry packages, and to do nice things for her from time to time. You see, she had a similar upbringing and custom was more on her side. So she actually was more convinced of her right to being pampered than he was.

Their marriage was stormy. They fought incessantly over who was supposed to do what for whom. Naturally things got worse and worse as each expected to be treated in marriage as they had been as children. It simply did not work. Two years later they divorced, still not realizing what had happened.

YOU DENY YOUR NORMAL RIGHTS

Self-assertion is not the same as grandiosity. You need not feel that every time you stand up for your rights you are acting like a tin god. Too many people think that satisfying their own ends makes them selfish. Think for a moment what that means. If you don't get your way, someone else is getting his or her way. How can it be otherwise?

You are being grandiose when you:

1. *Demand* that things go your way. That's frequently what dictators and bullies do. They don't ask for what they want. They tell you what they want.

If you aren't demanding that you get your way and if you aren't angry because others get their way, don't accuse yourself of being grandiose.

2. Not only demand that people bow and scrape before you but punish them if they don't. Parents do this to children, and mates do this to each other.

A father whose daughter had considerable talent at the piano wanted to control her training so much that she couldn't think for herself. He chose her instructors, which pieces she was to play, and a host of other things. He insisted on running every aspect of her life so she could become as famous as he always wanted to be.

That father was grandiose. He had to be to go through life thinking he knew more than everyone else. The girl finally had a breakdown because she simply couldn't live through him. The breakdown was her way of asserting her rights, it was her feeble way of fighting back.

3. Typically dominate others and feel superior to them. It isn't an occasional thing, it's almost all the time. Observe ten years from now, or back ten years, and you'll see a continuous pattern of relating to others in an I-am-superior-to-you attitude.

All of us get big ideas from time to time. Who has not thought I am right and the world wrong? And who has not thought of what I would do if the power were at hand to do it? But these are only grandiose fantasies which we entertain with tongue in cheek. As often as most of us get our way we give in to others' wishes. That's hardly grandiosity.

Therefore, consider seriously next time the issue arises whether or not you have the right to have your rights. Don't conclude that you're being a dictator if you think abstract painting is superior to traditional painting. You're still not being grandiose even if you buy only abstract art for your home as long as you allow your mate to buy traditional, if that's what he or she prefers.

In a society that tries to be fair it is only right that you gain your rights part of the time. Try not to feel guilty over that. As long as you aren't demanding that you get your way, or forcing your way on someone, or doing this almost exclusively of any other considerations, you're on the right course.

YOU *CAN* CHANGE

If you agree that you can be nice to a fault, you have made the first step in changing your personality. But to know you want to change is not enough. The difference between the persons who get respect and those who get stepped on is not what they usually say to themselves. Most cowards talk bravely from time to time, just as the hero does. So what's the difference? The difference is that the strong personality means what he or she says, the passive personality doesn't.

In the following chapters you will learn how to *mean* what you say or do. After reading this book, practice what you've learned. Become more assertive gradually. Don't take on your boss the first day. That's too much of an assignment at the start. Only after you've talked up firmly to the newsboy, the schoolchildren crossing your lawn, then the janitor at the school or in your office building or shop, can you gradually develop your skills at being a mature adult. Slowly but surely you'll get the practice needed to talk up to fellow employees, people over you, and people you love. All this can come in time if you believe that people can change if they know how to change and what to change. The clients I refer to are real. The identifying facts about their cases have been altered. But the gist of the problems and how the clients dealt with them are accurate.

As I always say, if Bill could learn to back up what he said and wanted to do, practically anybody can.

OBSERVATIONS OF PASSIVE PEOPLE

Out of my experiences with thousands of passive people, there are six observations I want to make. All these observations do not apply to all the clients I have observed, obviously. However, *some* apply to all the clients, and all the observations apply to *some* of the clients.

Observation 1: A TOTALLY PASSIVE PERSONALITY IS A RARITY.

Everyone, no matter how meek, is a strong and assertive person if given the proper circumstances. You may see yourself as weak and fearful in the presence of military officers, bosses, or parents and therefore conclude that you are an unassertive person. Nothing could be farther from the truth. Under the right circumstances you can and *will* straighten your back and fight the devil himself if he touches a sensitive spot in your life.

For example, do your knees shake when your superior bawls you out? You have to take his guff you say? Can't stand up or you may lose your job? Well, what would you do if this same boss started to beat you up? Or said vulgar things about your mother? Or took a sledgehammer to your car? Or struck your children? Or made a sexual overture toward your mate? Or burned your house down? Would you be passive in these situations? Hardly. In all likelihood the moment any of those events occurred you'd forget about your job, his feelings, his approval of you, or any other concern you may once have had. Suddenly you'd become assertive, not because that would be a totally new behavior for you but because you had been pushed to your limit of tolerance.

That's the basic problem with unassertive people: they have a high level of frustration tolerance, too high for their own good. They suffer put-down and abuse too long before they finally get enough of it and decide to rebel just as anyone else would. The difference between the passive and the nonpassive person is a matter of timing.

The assertive person gets fed up rather quickly when being taken advantage of. The unassertive person rebels too late, after suffering lots of abuse, but eventually rebels just the same.

You are already an assertive person. If you are being walked on, it's because you wait too long to do something about your frustrations, not because you can't do something about them.

Observation 2: PASSIVE PEOPLE ARE DOMINATED BE-CAUSE THEY ALLOW IT.

Children, the sick, and the aged are the only exceptions to this rule. In the final analysis, we cooperate with our aggressors because we hope to gain an advantage. The student who wants a good grade doesn't disagree with the teacher. The secretary does not slap the boss's face, because she wants her job. The housewife who has five children, few skills, and a wife beater for a husband suffers in silence because she has at least some security under his roof.

Such compromises are extremely common. We see people not asserting themselves almost every day. The notion, however, that they have no choice in the matter is a mistake. You and I always have a choice as to whether someone is going to make a mess of our lives. When we think the abuse is bad enough we will not hesitate to fight being abused. It is at that moment that the student will speak up to the teacher, ready to risk a failing grade or even expulsion from school.

The day also comes when the secretary slaps her boss for his indignities and decides to seek another job. And it's the same with the poor and beaten housewife. Eventually she too gets her fill and decides she'll have no more. Even if he might kill her, she is now ready to stand up for her rights. People have died for their principles throughout history rather than be dominated. That's what the Romans found out when they threw the Christians to the lions.

Observation 3: THE PERSON DICTATING YOUR LIFE LEARNED WHEN AND HOW TO DO SO BY YOU, THE VICTIM.

Have you ever wondered why many people you know are pushy, bossy, self-centered, and assertive whereas you are timid, shy, altruistic, and passive? Don't answer that question with the obvious statement that some people just are that way. That's too simple. The matter is much more complex.

Did you ever stop to realize that the passive pushover was taught to crawl by strong-willed people? Perhaps the child's mother or father praised their son for being a good boy only after he kept quiet and didn't hassle them. After years of rewards for being mousy, any red-blooded boy or girl is apt to wind up with the spine of a wet noodle. In other words, he becomes a doormat because his mother or father or some authority *trained* him to be one. They wanted him to be weak, they rewarded him for being passive, and they put him down for daring to develop in any other way.

Let's consider for a moment how Mr. Big Shot gets his personality shaped. Does he go to a school to learn to be a slave driver? I doubt it, because I've never heard of such a school. Does he read books on how to grind his heel into someone's back? There may be such texts, but I've never heard of one. There are plenty of books for bolstering your sagging ego, and books on how to sell whatever product you happen to be pushing. But they're not books that would literally teach you to get your way practically all the time at the cost of other people's frustrations.

Such books are not necessary, because you, the fearful one, are available. You, the constant peacemaker, are a friend of the bully. You, the doormat, are always there to provide a convenient place for someone to wipe his or her shoes on.

The gist of the matter is this: passive people are trained by aggressive people to be passive. However, these same passive people in turn are training the aggressive ones to be more aggressive. One trains the other. They couldn't live without the rewards each gives the other.

How, for instance, would a bully continue to dominate you if you simply refused to give in? How could angry and dominating people get their way if you didn't give them their way? Obviously they couldn't. A dictator is rewarded by weak and scared people for being mean and nasty. And the meaner and nastier he is, the quicker they hop to and do his bidding. So why should the bully change? He's got everything he wants. Now tell me, how in the world is he ever going to change when he gets payment of that kind? If he were sufficiently mature not to take advantage of his situation, he probably wouldn't have enjoyed kicking people around in the first place.

Doormats, stop licking the boot that's stepping on you. You are dominated because you allow it and even *teach* your bully to dominate you. Refuse to give Simon Legree what he wants and you'll begin training him to act more human. The world needs more strong but gentle people.

Take Etta, for example. She complained to me about how bossy her husband was.

"He always wants to tell me what to do and when I argue back he insists I didn't understand him. In the end I feel I have no rights to speak up and defend myself. Even when I do get a chance to put a word in edgewise, he won't let me finish my thought but says the rest of my sentence for me. You'd think I was a dummy or something."

"Have you ever had a quiet but serious talk with him, explaining how he acts and how you feel?" I asked.

"Of course I have. If I've told him once, I've told him dozens of times. I wonder sometimes if he's deaf, for all the good it does me."

"Then why do you suppose he doesn't change?"

"Beats me, doctor. It certainly isn't because he doesn't hear me. Must be something else."

How right she was and it didn't take me long to show

her what the trouble was. First I insisted that if his behavior continued despite her many complaints, it was because it was being rewarded. From somewhere he was finding out that if he cut her short and argued loudly enough, she would eventually give in. Why was I so certain of that? Because behavior that is not rewarded does not continue. It eventually dies off.

Etta's husband, on the contrary, was as pushy ten years after marriage as he was the first year. That could mean only one thing. He was being trained to be pushy, and guess who was doing the training. Tearful, exasperated, and confused Etta. It was she all along who was indirectly responsible for his pushy and inconsiderate behavior.

Here's how it worked. She would want more money for home expenses, let's say. He would disagree. Then she'd try to defend her viewpoint but he'd cut her down, interrupt, overpower her with words, and presto, Etta shut up.

That last act, Etta's keeping her mouth closed after he yelled at her, made him see (perhaps without being aware of it) that yelling and interrupting were very efficient techniques for getting his way. When Etta gave in after he got hot under the collar she fixed it so that he would very likely get hot under the collar again the next time he wanted his way.

Had she simply gone to the store and written out a check for what she needed, he would have realized that trying to outshout her would never work. In fact, if she made it a point to spend more when he was more difficult, she might have trained him to quiet down fairly soon. Look for that behavior which actually encourages someone to abuse you.

The next case study, of Emily, shows clearly how a mother was training her son to annoy her. Emily was a bright and loving mother, but her son was always a jump ahead of her. I asked her to explain why her nine-year-old was able to dominate her, a grown woman.

CLIENT: Well, he just constantly keeps at me. I try to outlast him, but he just keeps at me and keeps at me and he gets me so upset to the point where I just want to scream. Then I say: "Okay. Do it. Just leave me alone." He does. He is only nine years old but he knows. Sometimes he just wants to push me as far as he can. And he does. I know I let him. I know I do. I try to hold out, but I can't because he keeps at me.

THERAPIST: Why do you suppose he keeps at you?

C: I suppose he knows that in the end he will win. On the other hand, I am saying: "No, you are not going to win. You are not going to win."

T: You mean, not this time.

C: Yes.

T: And what actually happens?

C: He always does. Because he seems to have more persistence than I do.

T: Can you match him for half a dozen times or a dozen times, really match him and sweat it out for as long as it takes? And if he doesn't give in to you and if he gives you a bad time, can you send him to his room?

C: Well, I did that, but he goes in there and cries and talks real fresh to defy me.

T: Can't you knock on the wall and tell him that if he keeps it up he's going to stay longer?

C: Yes. I threatened to spank him, but he just keeps at it. It seems that's what he wants. I have even said to him: "You know, it doesn't have to be this way. You must enjoy it, because this is what you push me to."

T: No, no, no. I don't think he enjoys it. He's just absolutely convinced that he is on the right track. And he is. Because if he keeps it up, he *is* going to win. He has been reassured time and time again by *your* behavior, by your giving in to him. So why should he change?

C: I know, but it's hard for me to try to hold out, to develop more patience than he does. He seems to have it, you know.

T: Okay. Now I want you to put him in his room when he starts giving you back talk. Tell him he is going to stay there fifteen minutes or half an hour. All right? Now if that doesn't work, then next time add five minutes to it.

C: When he knows he is going there he will mumble to me and I will say, "If you've got something to say, say it." Then when I go to ask him he won't say anything. He will wait until I walk out of the room, then he will start up again.

T: Don't you see how he is baiting you?

C: I know he is. Why does he do that?

T: Because he wants to drive you to the point where you'll say: "I've had enough of this. Get out of here. Go to the ball game. Go to the movie, or do whatever you want."

C: Then when I ask him to do anything—I mean the simplest thing—it doesn't matter if he minds doing it or not, he'll make a comment, something simple. I could have just given him something, or taken him someplace he wanted to go, or done something with him. And I can turn around and ask him something so simple and I get, "Uh-h-h-h."

T: Yes. And then what do you do about that?

C: Most of the time I just say: "Never mind. If that makes you feel better, fine."

T: Okay. So why should he change? He doesn't even have to earn a gift or reciprocate a favor. You let it go and you wonder why the next time you want a favor from him he doesn't give you one. You are training him not to give in to you. The next time say: "Okay, I am not going to do you a favor when you want something. Next time you want an ice-cream cone I am not going to give it to you. And for being so uncooperative I am going to put you in your room for fifteen minutes." Now when he is in the room, if he bangs on the walls or wails loudly, tell him, "Because you are banging on the wall or because you are wailing loudly you are going to stay in another fifteen minutes."

C: But you see by that point I am just ready to go in there and—

T: I know, but that is exactly what he wants. He wants you to get so upset that you can't stand it anymore. That is exactly what he wants. I don't want you to give in to that temptation.

C: Okay. Then he cries and he cries. He isn't crying, but it is just as annoying as crying. Then I try to go in—

T: Don't do that. That's manipulation. He knows you much better than you know him. He knows that you are going to come in there and then he's got you right where he wants you. He wants you to feel guilty until you say: "Okay. Come on out. Give me a kiss." Then he has won again. I want you to get the kind of behavior from him that you are looking for. To do that, put

him in his room and leave him there until you get it.
Then you say, "Okay, now you can come out."

C: He may be there all night.

T: That's right. Let him stay there all night long. That
will happen only a few times. Once he realizes that
he can't manipulate you anymore, can't make you
give in to him, it will all stop in a hurry. Don't you see
that?

C: I do. It's doing it. It's getting to that place. I always
intend to and I really am going to.

Observation 4: PASSIVE PEOPLE USUALLY SUFFER
FROM ONE OR MORE OF THE FOLLOWING FEARS:

Fear of injury
Fear of failure
Fear of hurting other people's feelings
Fear of rejection
Fear of financial insecurity

These fears are so strong among passive people that
the next chapter will be devoted wholly to understanding them. They form the five major causes of passivity.

Observation 5: ACTS OF ASSERTION DO NOT IMMEDI-
ATELY IMPROVE RELATIONSHIPS. THEY MAKE THEM
WORSE.

If you have been a coward all your life and suddenly
begin to develop a backbone, what effect do you think
this great change is going to have on people in your life?
Are they going to step aside as you come through the
door? Are they going to stop in the middle of their

conversations so they can listen to every word you utter? Or will they be wonderfully agreeable and fair when you make a request that's going to put them out a bit?

They'll do none of these lovely things. In fact, after you begin to claim your rights, they won't even remain as nice to you as they were before.

Most people get nastier when you begin to expect fair and equal treatment. That may not be pleasant to learn, but it's the truth. Try it. Stand up firmly to someone who has been dominating you and watch what happens. You'll be accused of carrying on a revolution and immediately there will be a great huff as though you're the most unreasonable person in the whole world.

A client whom I shall call June complained bitterly about her husband's control of the purse strings. Since he earned the money, he figured he had complete right to control it. He would not listen to her argument that she earned some of that money too because he'd have to pay all sorts of people to do the many things she did if she weren't there.

Old Tight Fist didn't see it that way and continued to do the grocery shopping for her. He'd give her enough actual cash to fill the car with gas, pick up the cleaning, and perform other such duties, but he never relaxed enough to trust her judgment with money. She, of course, was unwittingly encouraging him to be like this because she allowed him to treat her like a child.

When she tried to put her name on the checking account he exploded. He yelled, shook his fist at her, and the next day requested the bank to keep the account under his name only.

She next took on a part-time job. This was going to

take her out of the home three evenings a week, requiring him to stay home with the four kids. He felt rudely put upon and decided to get even by going hunting and fishing every weekend, leaving her alone with the kids.

In the meanwhile June wasn't earning enough money to buy some clothes she needed for her job and lover boy wasn't about to write her out a check. So she sold a living room chair for a hundred dollars and bought the clothes herself. That did it. He now realized he had met his match and that he'd have to make concessions to his "crazy wife."

They talked and he grudgingly gave in to her conditions. She promised not to sell any more furniture, he promised to put her name on the checking account. She promised to quit her job if she could buy groceries and things and not have to account to him for every cent.

During this ordeal June was ready to throw in the towel a number of times. I reminded her constantly that things get worse before they get better when you force changes on people who are not used to them. It was largely for this reason that she stood her ground even though at times it felt like an earthquake. Had she done less, she would simply have trained him to be more unreasonable and in the end she would not have accepted that. *Divorce was averted because she was willing to face the storm for a while.* In the long run that was less uncomfortable than giving in to him would have been. Had she not made waves, the problem would have gotten worse and she would have had to rebel someday anyway.

If the person who is frustrating you is mature and understanding, there will not be a difficult time when you press for a change. That person will see the fairness in your complaint and try to accommodate you as quickly as possible. Little or no stress is created in such instances.

However, the story is different if your frustrater is hardheaded and downright immature. It is at that point that some of the worst storms happen between two people. A series of events are likely to follow when you stand up for yourself which can rip apart a friendship, a family, or a marriage. This predictable course of events need not surprise you. It happens so often you can even consider it normal. Here is an example of how it goes.

When Bertha heard that her daughter, Agnes, was going to leave college in her senior year she hit the ceiling. The mother had sacrificed for years to give her daughter a fine education and she wasn't going to take this decision lightly.

Agnes, however, had become a nervous wreck trying to live up to the mother's high expectations and was told by her school counselor to take a year off for a rest. Then she could return to her studies and finish up with her nerves intact.

Could Agnes hold out against the tactics the mother was ready to throw at her? She could if she knew what happens when people want to change the *status quo* against the wishes of the dominant person.

First Bertha yelled at her daughter and tried to reason with her. Agnes fought back day after day. Finally Bertha saw the futility of that maneuver and ceased her quarreling.

Then Bertha came on with a second tactic: she wept and pleaded and tried to make her daughter feel guilty. "Don't you realize all I've done for you? I only want it for your sake, really. I don't want this for me."

Agnes almost gave in on this strategy. But the thought of another year of hard study was more than she could accept and this helped her remain firm.

The third move by the mother was to threaten total rejection. "No daughter of mine is going to run off into the sunset and make a joke of all my work and dreams. If you do this, I'll disown you."

Before employing her final plan, she tried to discredit Agnes' school counselor. If she could make her daughter question the soundness of her therapist, Bertha had a chance of weakening Agnes' resolve.

This is not unusual with clients who are getting therapy. The party back home who is being frustrated by the new expectations of the client in therapy takes a serious dislike to the "head shrinker," who is "ruining" his or her life. The wife, husband, or parent not in therapy often tries in numerous ways to make the therapist look like a chump.

Agnes didn't bend.

The final strategy and the most powerful was for Bertha to threaten suicide. "What's the use? You spend a lifetime trying to accomplish something decent for your children and they ignore all your efforts. I give up."

This sometimes happens when one person wants to control another. If you give in anywhere along the line, you lose the struggle and will have to assert yourself again another day. If you stand firm and don't let yourself be dominated by one strategy or the other, you will be exposed to increasing discomfort but may well see the day when the pressure ends. Pain is usually unavoidable whether you protest or not. When you assert yourself, however, you experience less pain in the long run.

Bertha did not kill herself. Agnes took off a year for a much-needed rest and eventually returned to school and earned her degree.

This process of things getting worse before they get better I call "the Cold War." It can last anywhere from a few minutes to years. Each person in the struggle is fighting for what he or she believes to be a fair benefit. Sometimes negotiations help them reach acceptable compromises. Outside persons can be called in to help: friends, family, the minister, the family doctor, the family attorney, and perhaps (too late) your friendly therapist.

The important point is that change generally brings on some degree of suffering. And this suffering brought on by the Cold War can eventually lead to the Break, that point where the relationship ends. This is reached when neither party wants to compromise.

Most conflicts can be smoothed over through compromise. The laborer wants a dollar an hour raise, the employer would agree on fifty cents. They settle on seventy-five.

But suppose a married man wants a homosexual relationship. He's not likely to get a compromise. Most wives would insist on complete fidelity or the relationship is over. Even if he protests that he doesn't have to have two lovers as he had originally hoped, his offer of a compromise of one isn't going to appear fair in his wife's eyes. She is likely to insist on having her way totally or their struggle will deteriorate to the break-off point.

If the couple can compromise before the break and

the partners can feel reasonably content with the benefits they expect, the relationship is saved. If one party is made miserable while trying to make the second party content, that relationship will usually terminate. And it is good that this happens. Two persons do not belong together if they have to take turns being happy or miserable while trying to please each other.

Observation 6: EARLY ATTEMPTS AT ASSERTION ARE OFTEN CRUDE AND UNFAIR.

When you decide to stand up for yourself don't expect to be smooth at it. You'll be awkward for many trials. You may even be unfair and abusive of others as you try to learn these new skills. I've seen proper and dignified persons act with such poor taste when first asserting themselves that they shocked themselves into going back to their passive ways.

Some begin to use foul language after a lifetime of only civil speech. Some are downright rude and unreasonable as they try to make others treat them fairly. As far as the pendulum has swung to the passive side you may expect it to swing that far toward the aggressive side.

Be not dismayed. The skills you will learn are complex. To decide what is a fair course of action, to control your fear or anger as you reach the moment of truth, and to act upon that decision in a polished manner can all be learned, but seldom quickly. Each of these segments requires separate learning, then the three aspects require a coordination and blending that can also come only from experience.

Practice is the solution, practice plus the *careful* analysis of your course behavior. Self-damnation is a wasteful practice at this point. Don't regret asserting yourself even when you do it poorly. Analyze what you did wrong and try to correct it the next time you have an opportunity in a similar situation.

If you are one of those passive persons who is starting out badly, let me make two helpful suggestions: first, stand up for yourself in many minor ways before you take on the big issues. Second, assert yourself almost every reasonable chance you get, realizing that you may look like a buffoon. You did the same when you started to learn to roller skate, ride a bicycle, ice skate, or dance. You looked like a clumsy oaf when you began each of these skills. You kept on trying, nevertheless. Overcoming your awkwardness while skating on the thin ice of interpersonal relationships requires no less risk-taking.

No matter how long you've been shy and passive, you can change. If you work hard at understanding your behavior, the day *can* come when you'll be able to take command and give orders. Just because you have a history of scraping and bowing like a whipped slave, don't think you must forever kiss someone's foot. Change *is* possible for you, as it was possible for the millions who now know better.

I have seen angry husbands become mild and tender the day after they were told their wives wanted divorces. Terrorists have wound up holding Bible classes, and concentration camp commanders have been known to work as aides in hospitals for the terminally ill. Changes of the most fantastic kind are possible. Believe it! If that weren't true, there would be no reason for all the teachers in the world. The psychologists, the psychiatrists, and the ministers would all be wasting their time. The only reason counseling exists is that change is perfectly possible and always has been.

It's essential that you understand and believe in the ability of people to change or you'll never get your nose off the ground. Stop and think about your own life carefully and realize how very much you've changed already. And if you could make those changes, why not change other habits, such as letting people push you around?

Were you ever afraid to do something that now you feel comfortable doing? I know people who were terrified to speak in public but who do it quite easily now. Can you remember how awkward you felt at the thought of making love? Surely you don't feel that way today after years of marriage. Why is that? Simply because you can do an about-face in a great many endeavors.

Inability to change stems from the foolish notion that once something has affected you it must always do so. "You can't change a tiger's stripes," the old saying suggests, or "You can't teach an old dog new tricks" is another way this idea is expressed. Others insist: "It just isn't my nature. I've always been this way" and thereby give themselves the greatest excuse for remaining as they are.

Today you are what you convinced yourself of today. If you tell yourself today that you have no right to stand up for yourself, then you are going to knuckle under to everyone who barks at you. That may be what you've done all your life, but it doesn't have to be what you will do for the rest of your life.

Habits that you have had for years can be maintained

only by *thinking* about them in the future in the same way you thought about them in the past. Stop saying the same negative nonsense to yourself today and you will be able to wipe out a habit you have had since you were a child. Practically speaking, you won't succeed the first time you try. But if you do it over and over again, the day will definitely come when it will be mighty hard for you to allow anyone to push you around again.

2

The Five Coward Makers

Almost all passive people suffer from one fear or another. Without fear they would all be giants. The correction of poor assertiveness is therefore directly tied to becoming more fearless. The equation goes something like this: as fear diminishes, assertion increases. My book *Overcoming Worry and Fear* contains a fuller understanding of how we make ourselves afraid and what we can do to erase our fears.

FEAR OF INJURY

The crudest way to control others is by force. The big fellow pushes the little one around. Where does an eight-hundred-pound gorilla sleep? Anywhere he likes. Doesn't that nicely express the power of power?

Think over your own relationships with strong and potentially violent people. Don't you get out of their way, or argue less loudly because you could get smacked if things got out of hand?

No doubt about it, the fear of being hurt intimidates most of us. So what is the weaker person to do? One surely can't be run over by everyone who has a ten-pound advantage. I believe there are several solutions to this problem, not all of them are good, but they're better than a broken nose.

1. Learn how to talk your way out of a fight. Without kissing the other person's foot, you can often make your point and do it in such a pleasant and inoffensive way that the stronger person will not want to resort to violence. Often people engage in slugging matches because they've run out of talk.

I know an assertive man who weighs ninety-seven pounds. He insists he has not had a fistfight since he was seven years old. Even so, he has self-confidence, is practically never pushed around, and gets his way with potential bullies as often as larger men do. How does he do it? He speaks politely to them. He smiles, tries to be friendly and warm, and gives them nothing to get furious about. Still he gets his point across. He isn't wishy-washy even though he is gentle and polite.

I spoke to him on this issue and asked how he managed all his life to be so efficient at getting his way without running into a fight.

"I knew I'd lose any fight I ever got into. So I decided I'd have to choose my company and stay away from troublemakers whenever possible. Violent and unreasonable people scare me. I stay clear of them. I always pay close attention to how steamed up the other fellow is getting. When his temperature rises, I walk away or I become more diplomatic. One thing I never do at that moment, and that's to get insulting. That's like asking for a black eye."

There you have it in a nutshell. Do not throw gasoline on someone else's fire. Someone once said, "The beginning of wisdom is silence." That's great advice, especially at those times when the other person is rapidly reaching the boiling point.

2. But what if this psychology doesn't work? Two choices are before you if you are physically attacked: send the person to jail, or to the mental hospital. Call the police for your protection, make your complaint and don't worry about the threats you may get. It is much more important that you show determination and strength than that you worry about what might happen to you later. If you show weakness at a time when you had better show strength, you may not be around to worry about what will happen when that person is released.

3. Lastly, if all else fails and you're being attacked and you fear for your health or life, fight like a wildcat. Use anything you can to protect yourself in the same way you would protect yourself from a vicious dog. Self-defense has always been recognized as a valid reason for injuring an opponent. Don't feel guilty, try not to feel fear, simply defend yourself the best you can and hope it works.

FEAR OF FAILURE

It's sad how often people keep ideas to themselves and won't talk up simply because they fear doing poorly. This often leads to an invitation to let others dominate.

A husband and wife are buying a house. They see one she likes but he doesn't like it. But he won't say anything against it. Maybe his wife is right and it would be a good investment. What if he disagrees and later it turns out they made a big mistake? Instead of expressing himself openly he shrugs his shoulders, smiles weakly, avoids the possibility of making a mistake, and lets his wife do as she wants.

From this seemingly innocent series of events follow several predictable conditions. First, the husband is going to feel worse shortly after he decides to do nothing. It is said that not to decide is to decide. Instead of escaping trouble by avoiding making up his mind, he creates trouble. He'll feel guilty over being weak and over not saying what he means down deep. Then he'll hate himself and later hate his wife. All this for what? Because he was afraid he might be wrong.

Little does he realize it would be less painful to make errors, even real bloopers, than to avoid standing up for himself and making waves once in a while.

Sometimes we don't assert ourselves because we don't know what to say. We are simply speechless in some situations and it isn't merely because we are afraid of rejection or failure. We simply don't know how to speak up, especially with outspoken people. One of my clients once asked his fellow worker for a cigarette and got the following answer, "Tough luck, fellow, no way."

He was so taken aback by his rudeness he simply didn't know what to say. The remark was too unexpected for him to be prepared for it. So he walked off with an awkward smile when he really wanted to respond.

Don't be too upset when a thing happens that you never had to confront before. You're likely to stumble around and agree to conditions the first or second time it happens, but the day will certainly come when you can assert yourself after you've had that experience a few times.

The father of a teen-age girl answered the door one evening to find two seedy-looking fellows asking to come in to see his daughter. He immediately wanted to tell them to get lost but asked them in instead. Why? Because he was so surprised by them and their request he simply wasn't prepared. His final response was almost instinctive. Isn't it rude to let people stand outside in the cold while you stand there with your mouth open?

In his case he needed only one such experience to prepare him better for the next time. He determined to say and do what he meant and that was not let young men into the house unless they were expected by his daughter and she had notified him they were coming.

If you want to be in control of your life, don't be terrified of making poor decisions, just be concerned. Then, take the risk, stick your neck out and see if it gets chopped off. Seldom will that happen. On the contrary, you'll begin to develop confidence in your decision-making powers because of the wide experience you'll be getting. Mistakes are important: they teach you what to avoid, and that's something you may not have known before.

FEAR OF HURTING OTHER PEOPLE'S FEELINGS

If I can make you feel bad, worthless, and guilty because you won't do me a favor, I will have the same control over you a jailer would have. Your body and soul would belong to me. Guilt is one of the most frequently used techniques for controlling others. It succeeds so well because it hits deeply at your self-respect and leaves you feeling inferior to boot. A great weapon, watch out for it.

Mothers and fathers have ruled their children from distances of thousands of miles merely by suggesting that what the children do hurts their parents.

If you feel like a dirty dog when a loved one wants you to feel guilty, fight that feeling with all your might. Consider the following reasons for defending yourself.

1. You are a human being and a sinner. So what do people want of you, perfection? They aren't perfect. Where do they get off insisting *you* must be?

2. Those who lay guilt on you aren't being all that righteous as they'd have you believe. They may want you to think they're purer and superior to you. Don't buy that for one instant. What's so good and pure about anybody who *wants* you to feel like dirt? That's superior behavior?

When someone threatens to get upset or even to commit suicide unless you knuckle under, you're being blackmailed, *emotionally blackmailed.* This can be the most gripping kind of control a person can experience.

Mothers and fathers have been known to control their children by threatening to have heart attacks, to fall into depressive states, or to kill themselves if they didn't get their way.

Many times in my professional career I've had to counsel a young man or woman who wanted to break up a romance but felt too guilty to do so. In one recent example it was the girl who assured her boyfriend she would overdose if he left her. This froze him in his tracks. Obviously he couldn't break away if he was truly responsible for her misery.

"But that's the point, Richard," I responded. "You

won't make her miserable or upset or cause her to kill herself. *She* would be doing that to herself, you wouldn't be doing it to her. You can actually hurt people only physically, not psychologically. Your girl is talking herself into a disturbed state. And that's her problem, not yours."

"That may be so," he answered without thinking carefully about my comment. "But suppose she does try to kill herself. How am I supposed to live with that?"

"I just told you, Richard. How can you blame yourself for something she would have done to herself? If you put a gun to her head and pull the trigger, you're responsible for her death. If she puts the gun to her head and pulls the trigger, she's responsible. Get it?"

"Sounds awfully callous, if you ask me."

"It is callous. But it's a lot more callous to let her threaten you with suicide by letting her see how she's getting to you. You are encouraging her to use those threats more intensely each time. Unless you start becoming indifferent to her manipulations, she may really try to impress you with a genuine suicidal attempt. That's callous too, wouldn't you say?"

Richard thought a moment and took a new direction. "Even if I could agree with you, is that fair to treat someone like that who loves me so much?"

"What? Loves you so much?" I asked in amazement. "How do you figure she loves you? She's blackmailing you emotionally. She knows you'll suffer as though you were frying and you call that love? Who needs it?"

The conversation went on for a while in that vein until he could see how he had a right to change his romantic preferences and that a threat to blackmail him was a most hostile and unloving act. It was then that he broke the control that emotional blackmail and its accompanying guilt had on him.

3. Granted, you may *be guilty* of unkind, thoughtless, or stupid behavior but don't confuse that kind of actual guilt with *feeling guilty.* The latter means that you are personally worthless, no good, and evil because you have been less than perfect. *Being* guilty simply means you recognize that you've made mistakes. People can hardly control you body and soul if they point out your faults. But they can destroy you if you let them brainwash you into believing you are covered with invisible filth because you are actually guilty of misbehavior.

Let's take an example. You may have misplaced ten dollars and you would then *be guilty* of carelessness. We could say you are a careless person, you don't pay attention to details, you daydream. All these statements could be quite accurate. However, it would be totally wrong to conclude that you should *feel guilty* and wicked because you are careless. If that were true, we would all be worthless most of the time, since we all have faults. Separate your behavior from yourself and you can escape being controlled by people who want you to hate yourself. My book *Overcoming Depression* explains this point and technique in considerable detail.

4. You can't *make* anyone feel guilty or upset over what you do or don't do. This is perhaps the most important realization you will absorb if you want to conquer being controlled by guilt. You have never made your father, mother, wife, or husband feel guilty, aren't making them feel guilty now, and can't ever make them feel guilty. And they can't do it to you unless you allow it. We can talk ourselves into being guilty and upset. Your parents or mates talk themselves into being disturbed

over your frustrating behavior, while you talk yourself into being guilty over the pains they gave themselves. Children, because they are inexperienced and helpless, also upset themselves, but we can hardly expect more of them. As far as adults are concerned, however, your guilt comes from your head, not from the mouths of others. Grasp that idea and you control guilt feelings forever and the hold others have over you.

If you can make someone feel guilty over an act, you have control just as surely as if you held a gun in your hand. Most of us feel extremely uncomfortable with guilt and usually give in to others rather than live with this deep pain. If this has been a problem with you, learn how to think about this in a way that can enormously reduce control by guilt.

First, realize that you have a right to your views and desires. So does everyone else. Therefore, why must you feel guilty for what you want or think merely because another person disapproves?

An acquaintance of mine told me once that she gave away her food mixer. Her daughter came home from college and was about to whip up a batch of cookies when she discovered that her mother's very well equipped kitchen actually had no mixer. The mother had made thousands of cookies in her life and never much cared for the task. But, being a good mother and knowing what was expected of her, she kept on whipping up batches of cookies for years until one fine day she came up against the truth. "I have everything: house, marriage, children. So why am I so miserable?" When she realized how much of a slave she had been to that machine because others expected it of her, she rebelled and got rid of it. At first she felt guilty for being so selfish, but that wore off. When she spoke to me about it at a party it was something to laugh about.

So, marry whomever you think best. If your decision upsets your parents and friends, tell them to go see someone about *their* troubles. Do not let them talk you into believing that it's your responsibility to solve their disturbance.

Martha was having a serious problem with her grown daughter. The girl would visit her mother only after drinking heavily and would then come banging at the door at three in the morning. After a while Martha overcame her guilt and at the point of an umbrella told her child to stay away until such time that she could visit under sober conditions and with good manners.

"I've wanted to do that for years," she explained, "but the guilt would have killed me. As a result I was never as firm as I could have been and now my girl is spoiled and has no respect for me. If I had known years ago that her rejection didn't have to hurt me and that I had a right to frustrate her for her own good, I'd have stood up to her then. Now I know that I don't have to feel guilty when I say no. I don't hurt her feelings when I don't give in, *she* does."

The daughter had the option of remaining upset because she wasn't getting her way, or she could learn some psychology as her mother had and thereby conquer her problem from *inside,* through her making deep personality changes rather than insisting her mother had to make *outside* changes in the problem itself.

Conquer your guilt over asserting yourself and you beat down a common cause of being a pushover. You'll want to be careful, of course, that you use good judgment as to how often you get your way. You could turn out to be a pretty unreasonable person yourself if you were not cautious with this knowledge.

FEAR OF REJECTION

The greatest fear you may have is the fear of disapproval. You were taught to think that rejection actually hurts and that you positively must be upset if you are rejected. Furthermore, you were taught that rejection proved something: that you were worthless, or why else would someone reject you?

It's easy to see how people will do almost anything for others if they think they'll be treated like lepers unless they dance to others' tunes.

We feel so strongly about having to be liked and loved that we do the most ridiculous things imaginable, all for the approval of someone else. Why else is Ms. Catch always having people over for dinner whom she hardly knows? This poor creature, so fearful of what others may think, can't say no to anything that is asked of her.

A new neighbor brought a dress over for advice as to how to hem it. Ms. Catch offered some suggestions and guess what happened. She pulled out her sewing machine and did the neighbor's work for her.

She was pleased that her neighbor was satisfied, but that feeling lasted only a short while. Beneath the pleasant smile she was doing a slow burn. And when the neighbor went home, Ms. Catch hated herself so much for allowing herself to be taken advantage of that she reached for her bottle and tried to drown her guilt in booze.

Fear of rejection is common among teen-agers. But

millions of adults also, who make decisions on employment, loans, jail sentences, and who run schools, colleges, churches, business, and industry still shake at the thought of being disliked by important people in their lives.

Lucy was a capable woman in her late twenties. She dressed well, had poise, and looked for all the world like a stable person. You can imagine my surprise when she complained about her mother's hold over her.

I asked her what her mother would do if she rebelled. Lucy couldn't even consider such an act. Well, I had heard that sentiment hundreds of times and knew just how to show her how wrong she was. I always present clients with outlandish abusive situations that even they would not tolerate. This demonstrates to them that they can be strong if they are pressured to do so.

So I smugly asked Lucy if she'd resist her mother if she tried to make a dope addict of Lucy's teen-age daughter.

Her amazing answer was "No." I couldn't quite believe what I had heard.

So I approached the matter again with another and even more disgusting example of abuse. Would she stop her mother from making a prostitute of her daughter?

"No." And she meant it.

"Would you stop your mother from whipping your girl severely with a belt?"

"She already does," was the reply, which left me stunned into momentary silence. Such lack of assertiveness I had not seen in years.

Some months later Lucy was seriously contemplating her mother's rejection for the first time in her life. Our conversation then was so to the heart of this matter of standing up for yourself that I quote it verbatim.

THERAPIST: What would your mother do if you told her to let you and your daughter alone?

CLIENT: She'd probably sit there with her mouth open. She'd get upset and hate me.

T: You're sure?

C: I'm positive.

T: What would she do, try to make you feel guilty?

C: Probably. She would probably start crying too.

T: She'd probably start crying, why?

C: Because of what I said. She'd let it hurt her.

T: She'd let it hurt her—right. Now do you think it's worth so much not to have your mother cry that you would give up growing up?

C: No.

T: Is it important enough to grow up even at the cost of having your mother cry?

C: Yes. I'm going to have to.

T: You don't have to, you know.

C: I want to grow up.

T: You'd better learn to stick up for yourself then.

C: I want to.

T: There's a price you have to pay for that. Do you understand that?

C: Yes.

T: What is the price you'll be paying?

C: Letting her hurt herself from what I have to say or do.

T: That's right. Can you stand that?

C: I can try.

T: Exactly. Try. Because if you don't, what's going to happen to you?

C: I'm going to be a little baby, scared of everything all of my life.

T: All of your life, yes. And then when she dies, then what?

C: I'm going to be lost.

T: Right. You're going to be lost.

Don't misread what I'm saying at this point. I've never said it wasn't important to have people like you or think well of you. Life isn't much fun if you're all alone and nobody cares whether you live or die. So despite what I pointed out above, I still insist that having an intimate relationship is one of the blessings of life. Few things bring us more contentment than do those we love and those friends whose companionship we treasure.

Having said that, I must emphasize that much of our misery in life comes when we make the approval of those close to us of compelling importance. To be sure, they *are* important, but don't ever believe for one moment that they are matters of life and death to you. When you let others walk all over you, that's precisely what you've done. You've made their approval so important that you have surrendered your self-respect, and without that, what is left to admire and love?

If you truly want to be important and loved by others, then stop believing you must do everything they want. Instead of striving so mightily for love, strive harder to get their respect. If someone doesn't respect you *first,* you're not likely to be loved later. That's the way it is with us humans. We can love pets and children without first respecting them. But we seldom do this for adults. Therefore, to secure the kind of love you've always wanted, learn to frustrate others when the issue is important to you and unimportant to them. Why should they get their way then?

If the issue is important to them but not to you, give in. That's only being decent. People who lack assertiveness, however, don't even recognize when an issue is truly significant for them and insignificant for others. A mother, for example, who has been on her feet all day and longs for a quiet moment in the evening has every right to tell her children she will not drive them to the ice-cream store. They don't need another dessert. They're not as tired as she is, because they haven't cleaned house all day. If they want it badly enough, let them use their bicycles or walk.

Too often, such simple acts of assertion are not maintained, because the mother doesn't realize how much more important it is for her to rest than it is for her children to be cheered up for ten minutes.

The children will probably protest against her self-interest and show her considerable displeasure. This is a normal response and need not be taken seriously. After all, if the children can tolerate not being loved and approved of by the mother for a few hours or a few days, isn't it reasonable to assume that she can tolerate it also? She's supposed to be the stronger and more mature person. And she is.

FEAR OF FINANCIAL INSECURITY

More people than you would believe remain on jobs they hate because they need the money. And more people than you would believe stay in unhappy or even miserable marriages because they need the money. The fear of going hungry or of being broke is reasonable to those people at the end of their rope. Men and women remain chained to miserable jobs and miserable marriages because either one at least keeps a roof over their heads and their stomachs full.

You can't blame them. Most of all, they want to live even if it isn't in grand style. However, the price for the roof overhead and bread on the table may be to knuckle under to an unreasonable parent, boss, or mate. A surprising number of marriages, in my experience, are kept together not by love but by money. Usually it is the female who is dependent on the male for his earnings. Unless she plays his games his way, she may find herself with her bags out on the street (or so she thinks).

I'm convinced there would be a rush on the divorce courts tomorrow if society could give women decent-paying jobs or give them enough money outright so they could keep house by themselves. What masquerades too often for love is nothing more than fear of being penniless or of having to reduce one's life-style drastically.

To avoid finding yourself in this trap, it is essential that you keep up your work skills and improve them when possible. Go back to school, take up better-paying work, save your money, and then when you find your situation unbearable, leave. You will have prepared yourself to the point where you can make it on your own.

The best things in life are *not* free. Clean air is not free, food is not free, medical services are not free, transportation, heat, clothing, and shelter, none is free. Neither is peace of mind. You pay for the good life with cash. The less of it you have, the more you're likely to suffer. The more of it you have (up to a point), the better your life and well-being are apt to be. Money *can* buy happiness, lots of it, in the form of rent payments, good food, trips, and an occasional bottle of wine. People who have the good things in life usually enjoy life more than those who don't have them.

Put aside your romantic notions of how sweet it is to smell the flowers. Unless you have eaten recently, you won't smell daisies, you'll eat them. Money is not the root of all evil, poverty is.

Therefore, if you are suffering under a dictator who holds the dollar sign over your head, don't make waves until you can be sure you can survive if you leave home, quit your job, or get your divorce. You may have to accept food stamps and welfare to make such a move, but that's up to you. When you're hurting enough you'll change your situation. But never do it unless you know you won't freeze or starve.

3

Excuses, Excuses

Rationalizations, those handy psychological tricks we use to get out of tight spots, come easily when we try to develop habits of assertiveness. This chapter describes most of the more common rationalizations we use to remain passive.

RATIONALIZATIONS AND ASSERTION

To get control of your life, it is imperative that you not make endless excuses why you cannot ventilate your grievances. Sure you're going to get scared when the moment of truth arrives. However, if you really want respect from your peers, if you want to stop feeling inferior and manipulated, you had better face this truth: you can never learn to assert yourself *unless you assert yourself.* If you weasel out of that task by making one rationalization after the other, you'll never conquer that bad habit.

You may say: "I don't dare speak up to my boss. He'll fire me." Nonsense. If that is literally true, then start looking for a new job right now, because you're sure to disagree with your boss again someday. If you must give in to his every wish in order to keep your job, you're wiser to *fire him.*

More importantly, your boss is not likely to fire you for disagreeing with him. He's more likely to develop a healthy respect for you. If you have a mind of your own, you will impress others with your self-confidence. The person at the top didn't get there by bowing and scraping. Any organization is careful to promote its most talented people, not only its most agreeable. And one way talent gets recognized is by its being expressed when a person is willing to take chances.

Another common rationalization is: "It's no use. I'm not going to get my way even if I am firm." If you believe that, really believe it, of course you're not going to try. And later, what are you going to say? That you were right? Probably. But can you see how you didn't actually *predict* the future, you *determined* it! That's like saying you're going to have body odor whether or not you shower. And then, believing that, you don't shower and later do smell.

If you want to stop people from putting demands on you and slice away pieces of your life, you had better take a positive attitude. You'll never know what you can achieve until you try. You are sure to succeed to some degree if you try. It's only when you don't try that you fail. Today, within the next few hours, stop your habit of living under another's expectations and, if it is important to you, do your own thing.

A third rationalization commonly given is: "I really wanted to do some assertion exercises this week but I didn't have the time or opportunity." Nonsense. There is always opportunity and time to practice something as important as saving your psychological hide. The waitress at the café was very slow in giving you a refill of coffee. Couldn't you have said something to her? And when the girl in the office answered the phone three times while talking to you, would it have been so wrong to tell her you were there before the three callers on the phone?

As you left the building you saw a blind man groping for the handle of the front door. A small group of adults waiting for the bus paid no attention to him. Wasn't that an excellent opportunity to help the blind man and then say something to the group about their neglect?

And, thinking in that vein, you could practice saying and doing what you mean all day long in literally dozens of situations.

No more excuses! There's work to be done. Go to it!

THE DIFFERENCE BETWEEN SELFISHNESS AND SELF-INTEREST

When I try to teach people to be good to themselves they get confused. They feel selfish (and guilty) on the one hand and unselfish (but frustrated) on the other hand. I have repeatedly made the point that relationships deteriorate rather than improve when you make excessive sacrifices to please the other person. Yet how can you do that if you feel like a cad for wanting your way and for deliberately frustrating someone else?

We must distinguish between selfishness and self-interest. This distinction is critical if you want to be a mature person and not let others abuse you. If you don't understand this distinction, either you'll feel uneasy for not doing your family a favor or you'll feel put upon because you've given in to them again. Here is how I define those two terms:

You lay back on the sofa propped up on a pillow tossing bonbons into your mouth, and give orders to your family to be quiet while they put on your favorite record, make your coffee, and open the window a bit so you can catch the cool breeze. That is being selfish, because you are expecting others to put themselves out exclusively for you with no expectation of your doing something for them. In other words, the selfish person wants something for nothing.

The self-interested person, however, may also want to rest on the sofa, eat bonbons, and want the same services but not actually be a selfish person, for there is every intention of doing something in return for those favors.

For example, what's selfish about wanting your wife to bring you a cup of coffee if you just did the dishes for her? And what's selfish about her asking you to do the dishes if she cooks the meal? And what's selfish about your asking her to open the window and to put on your favorite record if you have just come back from picking up the dry cleaning?

These are not selfish acts, they're acts of reciprocity, acts of payment for services rendered or expected. They say that you are important and so is your partner. Each of you deserves consideration. It is in this way that businesses, marriages, and neighborhoods get along smoothly. It is an arrangement you do not need to feel guilty about. If you value yourself, expect some recognition for most of your services. That doesn't mean, of course, that you need a medal for every favor you do. If you buy a poor kid a bag of popcorn, you'll only get a smile and a thank-you for it. However, when you're in close and prolonged contact with a person you surely can't be the one who is always contributing. You'll want repayment eventually even if it isn't exactly tit for tat. But it surely has to be reasonably so.

To feel guilty about wanting a kind deed returned is neurotic. It spoils the other person, makes you miserable if done often enough, and threatens to sour the marriage, the friendship, or the business relationship. To keep any of these arrangements healthy, be self-interested but not selfish. The time has come for us all to stop feeling guilty about wanting to please ourselves. It is right and moral that we behave self-interestedly some of the time, at least to the point where we are reasonably happy and our mates are reasonably happy. Is it wrong to be interested in yourself, your looks, your health, your advancement? Would you seriously suggest you have no right to clean clothes? That's self-interest. To a good meal? That's self-interest. To a shower or bath? That's self-interest. To a phone call from a friend? That's self-interest. And so on. To be self-interested is healthy and necessary if you want happy relationships with others. Whether you call it selfishness or anything like it is not as important as your realization that you are an important person, maybe not to everyone in town, but surely to yourself. And if you don't look out for your interests to a *reasonable* degree, usually no one else will.

PEOPLE ON PEDESTALS

Doing your own thing is often not easy. One of the most difficult hurdles to overcome to achieve self-determination is the fear of disagreeing with people whom we have placed high on a pedestal, particularly our parents.

You are taught to respect your elders and to honor your father and mother. Such teaching has great merit. Until such time that you are mature and capable of making sound decisions, often your best guidance comes from those teachers who care for you the most.

However, when are you old enough to think for yourself? Admittedly you probably need guidance in abundance during your teen years, but do you need constant supervision when you are eighteen? You do? Well, how about twenty? Still need it? Would you say twenty-five or thirty?

Believe it or not, occasionally I run across normally intelligent people who are in their thirties and forties and still afraid to disagree with their parents. They believe so strongly that disagreement means dishonoring that they give in to their parents on the most preposterous issues.

One man in his thirties was told by his mother that she expected him and his family over for the Christmas holidays. He, however, had just promised his wife that they would all go to her folks' home for the celebration. Now what was the poor fellow to do? To go against his mother's wishes would be disrespectful. He was an obedient son who honored and loved her. He did not want to hurt her feelings by rejecting her offer.

When he told his wife of his decision to go back on his word, the marriage was put under such strain they decided to get counseling. Here are some of the things I pointed out to the husband.

First, he needn't have felt guilty over his mother's

hurt feelings, because he could not have been responsible for them. Had she not felt sorry for herself over not getting her way, she could have tolerated the frustration even if she didn't think it was fair. If need be, he could even have referred his mother to counseling so she could be taught how not to react in such self-defeating ways.

Secondly, he needn't have equated disagreement with dishonor. If his mother had her way often in the past, it is only fair that his wife and her mother get their way too. His mother was simply wrong and selfish to demand that she have her way all the time. To go against her wishes does not mean her son dishonors her. Why can't he still love her and honor her for all the wonderful things she has done for him throughout his life despite the fact that he thinks she's wrong in this instance?

Thirdly, to treat her as though she were always right is to treat her like a goddess, like someone on a pedestal. She is not superhuman, she does not belong on a pedestal. To put her there does her enormous disservice. She is a human being just as you and I and makes the same unwise decisions we all do. That applies to your parents and to mine and I hardly think we love them the less for it.

Fourthly, to give in to your parents because you have to "honor" them makes spoiled and indulged persons out of them as a by-product. Few people can be treated like gods without letting that go to their heads.

Therefore, in your search for independence learn to say and do what you mean, even with loving parents and respected authorities. You *and* they will grow by it.

IF HE'S CONVINCED, HE MUST BE RIGHT

Another technique for dominating people which you may have observed a million times and not have been aware of—I even had to be reminded of it by one of my young clients—is to believe that a person is right because he or she is so convinced. This had been a lifelong problem with my client and her husband. The girl was no dummy, she could argue quite well, yet she was repeatedly giving in to the wishes of her spouse and feeling resentful each time.

I suggested that she was probably afraid to take a stand for fear she might be proved wrong. This is a frequent cause of backing down to others. However, she didn't think that accurately described her behavior. Then I insisted she was afraid to assert herself because he'd get angry and reject her, another extremely common cause of cowardly actions.

Again she felt that this explanation didn't quite hit the mark. After all, she was thinking of divorce even as we discussed this matter. The fear of rejection couldn't have been all *that* strong.

The young lady thought about it a few moments and in a flash of insight gave me the following explanation.

"I give in to Joe when we argue because he seems so absolutely sure of himself. When I come across anyone who acts like he'd bet his life on what he's saying, I automatically think I've got to be wrong. I don't think I'm ever that sure of myself. Therefore, when I come up against a stone wall I assume the person is not budging because he or she would be making a mistake to do so."

How right she was. I had seen this happen many

times in my life and in the lives of others. It isn't the smartest who get their way all the time by any means. It's often the fellow who convinces others that he's completely correct and that you'd be a fool to challenge him.

Harry made the statement at a party once that a streamlined airplane and an old-model airplane each traveling one hundred miles per hour into a head wind of ten miles per hour would end up flying ninety miles per hour. This happens to be true.

Pete contested this immediately. He could not be persuaded that streamlining an airplane would only allow it to fly faster with less energy than an older model needed. In his mind a head wind of ten miles per hour just had to hold back a snub-nosed plane more than a sleek model.

So convinced was Pete of how right he was that every man listening in the group agreed with Pete and thought Harry was just pulling their legs. That's how convincing Pete was.

Maybe you've been convinced of the wisdom of buying a house or a car and at your leisure wondered why in the world you did it. Then you recalled how absolutely convincing the salesman was. Why was he so convincing? Because he was certain he was right. Your doubts simply melted before the certainty of his beliefs. In a moment of weakness you were swayed from your logical position and before you knew it you were snowed.

Don't let someone's convictions delude you into thinking therein must lie the truth. Certainly that can be the case. However, often as not, fools are as certain as wise men. So the best course to follow is be aware of

your tendency to be convinced by an all-knowing attitude and to think over carefully *what* is being said, not
how it is said.

You'll be pleased to know that the young lady who
allowed herself to be brainwashed by a hard- and fast-
talking husband eventually learned to separate the
what he said from the *how* he said it and stood up for
herself thereafter.

I'M NOT EDUCATED

One neat way to rob persons of their self-respect and
then rub your heels into their self-image is to convince
them they don't know much because they're poorly
educated. This is the favorite method of educational
snobs who believe that anyone who doesn't have a degree from a prestigious college is a peasant. They learn
quickly that most uneducated persons are highly self-
conscious of their lack of education. Some are not only
self-conscious, but humble and humiliated, as though
they were somehow an inferior species. In that frame
of mind they can become the easiest pushovers in the
world.

First, they become sensitive of their poor English.
They use words incorrectly and mix up their tenses.
When people talk about Chaucer, Verdi, or ontogeny,
these persons feel uneasy and become silent. They feel
that they have no right to argue against those who have
had so much schooling. When this keeps up they eventually become bitter, defensive, and smart alecks or
they become passive, shoulder-slumped doormats.

These people never heard of concrete intelligence.
This is different from abstract intelligence, the kind

called for in reading and writing. Concrete intelligence is the kind required if you're on a camping trip and you get lost. Or if you have to pull the family through a critical period on a small sum of money. The fellow with concrete intelligence can take charge, give orders, make decisions, and use plain good sense. And that's something you don't learn in books.

I know of any number of men who are bright but uneducated and did not let themselves feel inferior. As a result they're successful, well adjusted, and happy. One of my neighbors made all sorts of grammatical errors when he spoke. But he was a millionaire and the president of a respectable company. And I've known Ph.D.'s who may have been experts on the migratory habits of the Siberian musk-ox but who could hardly find their cars after a movie. Then, too, let's never forget that many of the nations throughout history have been ruled by intelligent and educated monarchs, and those governments have long since disappeared. In fact, some of the worst pages in history were written during the reigns of highly educated kings and queens. Even today you can see by looking at local and federal governments that education is not a magic pill before which we must all bow. Bright people can be unstable, and uneducated people can be mature. It's maturity that often makes the important difference between a sound decision and a poor one. One of the brightest men I ever met was well read and highly educated but could not hold the simplest job. And I mean the simplest job, such as short-order cook, dishwasher, or dog-catcher.

I don't want to put down education. Despite what I've said, education is important for the eventual improvement of society. That hardly means, however, that anyone who has gone beyond high school is a blooming genius to whom others with less schooling must pay homage. I don't object to paying respect, but it will be for wisdom gained, not facts memorized, for maturity achieved, not power granted because of a degree.

Give in to the educated man, not merely because he's educated but because he's right (if he is). When he's not right, disagree with him as you would with your brother-in-law.

IT'S NO BIG DEAL

One of the most common reactions to any frustration is to interpret it as much more than it is. Get fired from a job and you're likely to think of it as the end of the world rather than as an annoyance. Get a flat tire and you're prone to think of it as a catastrophe rather than as a pain in the neck. Someone rejects you and you naturally think of it as a tragedy when it's only another one of those sad happenings that come into all lives at one time or another. All these disturbances could be reduced or eliminated if you would learn not to build mountains out of molehills.

Interestingly enough, doing the complete opposite doesn't assure you of the happiest existence either. If you consistently tell yourself that your present frustration "isn't a big deal," four actions usually follow. First, you'll become calm and undisturbed. Second, the frustration is likely to continue, since you are not doing anything about it. Third, you're going to feel dominated because someone is imposing frustrations on you which you're making no effort to resist. That's when the fourth action enters the picture: the slow burn. You'll begin to resent the whole business and lose your composure in the process.

Sarah roomed with her best friend, Frances. They got along quite well for the first two months. Then Sarah began to realize that Frances had a bad habit. She seldom cleaned the tub after bathing. Sarah didn't mind at first, but when it happened over and over she became irritated. Even after she mentioned it to Frances the habit continued.

To deal with this irritation she wisely told herself it was not a catastrophe to have a sloppy roommate. In this she was correct. However, she went too far in denying the frustration. She tried to convince herself it was not a frustration at all, and that was hardly accurate. When she said, "It's not a big deal," she was trying to convince herself it was not a frustration. That was her mistake.

There is no reason why we cannot admit that we are frustrated while not making a catastrophe out of it. That may be a narrow path to follow, but it's important to make that distinction. For instance, you won't die if your friend always shows up late for a tennis date. It's truly not a catastrophe. But it is a big enough thing anyway to justify saying or doing something about it. For example, you could leave after a specified period of time, say ten or fifteen minutes. Or not accept any offers for other games in the future.

The point I want to make is this: Why live with frustrations if you don't need to? They are irritating. They consume time and energy. A frustration requires that you give yourself therapy for as long as the frustration exists. Who needs it? Isn't it far more sensible to stop letting people run over you even though their actions are not catastrophic? I think so.

The next time someone steps in front of you in the movie line, don't let it pass by, thinking it's no big deal. Of course it's no big deal, but it is *irritating* and *unfair*. And if you don't do something about it, you'll be encouraging people to do that sort of thing again. And you'll be developing a bad habit: letting people take advantage of you. Unless you enjoy having others use you, I urge you to make a fuss, not a huge fuss, but enough of a fuss to correct the wrong. It will make your life easier in the long run. Sarah found out that Frances was too undisciplined for her, so she got another roommate. Bravo, Sarah!

I TOLD YOU SO

Making mistakes is part of being human. No one escapes. Still, have you ever wondered why you are so sensitive when you botch something after you were warned that you'd do that very thing? I'm referring, of course, to the "I told you so" complex.

It clearly proves that we are more sensitive to being *reminded* about mistakes than making the mistakes in the first place. So scared are we of having our errors thrown in our faces that we often fail to act. We let others have their way just so we won't be confronted with an "I told you so."

There is something so irritating, nasty, and demeaning about this little bit of behavior that most people react against it in what seems an instinctive manner. Certainly Sam did. His life was virtually dominated by his avoidance of an "I told you so."

He purchased stock on the advice of a friend who had often done well on the market. His wife didn't like the idea. She protested and warned him they'd lose their shirts. Sam listened and hesitated but after a few days decided to buy. Dreaming he'd make a killing, he contentedly went about his life with a slight smile and humming a tune. In two months he began to see how right his wife was. And she began to see it too. She told him so. Not once, but over and over.

"What right did you have to buy that worthless stock without my permission? Didn't I tell you it was a bad investment? You and your crazy ideas for getting rich."

Sam would let this kind of talk cut into his self-confidence. He learned his lesson, all right. He learned it so well that he never invested in stocks again. But that wasn't the end of it. When they bought a new car Sam thought a gas-saving model made good sense, so he suggested they get a small car. His wife wondered about how comfortable a small car would be but agreed with him that economy was the most important consideration.

Sam soon learned that his model was inexpensive not only because it was small but because it was not built for endurance either. First the brakes went, then the water pump, and so on. His wife was greatly irritated by these developments and soon picked on him for his bad judgment. Before long she was throwing "I told you so" at him even though she originally went along with the decision. She defended herself by saying: "I had my doubts all along but I didn't want to say anything. After all, the man *is* supposed to know about cars, isn't he?"

Sam eventually learned he could not win. If he made

good decisions, she took part credit for them. If he made poor decisions, he was branded a fool. So Sam played it safe. He took a back seat to his wife, did nothing unless he was positive it could not backfire, and let her run his life.

If this is your sad tale too, I suggest you get thick-skinned and learn to let the "I told you so" comments bounce off your hide. Anyone who uses that tactic repeatedly is insecure and immature. Such a person is no one to get upset over. Next time you goof up and you know you are going to be put down, remind yourself how some pathetic people can only feel "tall" if they stand on the bodies of others. Instead of putting their right foot on the victim and letting out a Tarzan call of the wild, they give forth with a loud, "I told you so."

IF YOU REALLY LOVED ME

Another way to make doormats out of people is through guilt. And one of the best ways to create guilt is to accuse persons of not caring for you, and you do this by appealing to their claims of love. "If you really loved me, you wouldn't object to my going hunting," he tells her. And she, feeling like a sinner, backs away from her request for companionship and lets him go.

Recently I was counseling a young lady who was quite fond of an airline pilot. She was getting serious over him and he liked her a great deal also. However, when he was in town he wanted the freedom of dating other girls and he expected to do this when he was flying out of other cities. She did not like the idea and gave him an ultimatum. "Either be loyal to me or forget our relationship."

He chafed at this restriction and came back with: "If you really loved me, you'd understand my needs. I'm not ready to settle down. Besides, I get lonely in Frisco or Houston. What do you expect me to do, watch television in my motel room each night?"

She asked me if she was being unfair to request fidelity of him. After all, he wasn't married to her, he had a right to date other women, and maybe she was being unloving to make such rigid conditions.

I suggested she consider the following: *(a)* True, he had a right to date others since he wasn't married. *(b)* So did she. Was he ready to let her date when he was out of town? No? Then he had no right asking for permission to date but not giving it also. *(c)* Since when was it proof of her not loving him because she didn't want to share him with others? Couldn't the exact opposite point be made? Couldn't she say, "If I really loved you, I would forbid you to chase other girls"? Why not? Surely that would show more caring than a sharing attitude would show. *(d)* Who said in the first place that giving in to the wishes of others proves your love? Since when? If your friend wants to drink poison, would you be proving your love if you gave him some? If your mate is an alcoholic going through a withdrawal period and begs on his knees for a drink, would you give him one? And if he threw that clincher, "If you really loved me . . . ," you surely wouldn't be taken in, would you? In fact, by proving your love as he would want you to, you could be harming him considerably.

The last item to consider, however, is that when someone wants to control you with "If you really loved me . . ." you have an equal right to say, "If you really loved me, you wouldn't make that request." What's good for the goose is good for the gander.

My client thought about these suggestions for several weeks. When next her boyfriend flew into town she was ready for him. The poor fellow ran into a buzz saw of objection. She countered each of his statements with an objection that was so logical he was speechless. When she finally confronted him with the notion that he would treat her a great deal differently "If he really loved her," he saw red. Losing his sweet composure, he flew into a rage, cursed her thoroughly for being a women's libber, and slammed the door behind him.

To my surprise my client was not upset over these developments. She quickly reasoned that anyone who would dump her the minute he realized he was not about to get his way completely wasn't worth crying over. She had been tolerant of his views in the past because she truly cared for him. But he was not the least tolerant of hers if they differed from his. Who needs a relationship like that?

You who are always ready to show your love to others, you cannot love anyone for long who simply takes from you and gives little in return. So, if you want love, it's a two-way street.

OTHER-PITY

To say and do what you mean is one of the most difficult things with which people struggle. Yet, if you want to be fair or simply efficient, you had better learn how to do precisely that.

Take the case of a young executive. He is unhappy over the way one of his secretaries waltzes into the office every day about ten minutes late. He knows full well that the other girls resent what she is getting by with and that they are beginning to sluff off on their own duties out of spite. He obviously wants to talk to the tardy office worker but doesn't. Why?

Because he pities her. She's sensitive and can't take criticism. In fact, she gets real moody when she's put on the carpet. Big, glistening tears roll down her rosy cheeks, and our young executive is simply too moved by such scenes to seek them out. The net result is that she continues to create a bad feeling in the office. Her boss feels guilty with himself for being so chicken, and the other employees resent the girl and lose respect for the boss. All because he has too much other-pity.

"Well," you ask, "what's a person to do? Aren't decent people supposed to be aware of the feelings of others? Isn't it right to show compassion for their suffering?"

Of course it is. However, we are more rational if we try to distinguish between compassion and pity. It's one thing to care for the welfare of a person, and quite another to pity that person. The young executive, for instance, is feeling so sorry for the girl that he is not helping her. She's learning bad office habits because he's letting her get by with them. He's concerned about only one small part of her welfare when he pities the pain she goes through from being called to account.

A truly compassionate person would look at the larger picture and not hesitate to act for the ultimate benefit she would gain by growing up and facing her responsibilities. Often, caring for someone is best shown through the expectations you place upon them and the discomfort you subject them to rather than through indulgence.

If you pity your child so much when he screams and kicks as he goes for his polio shot that you do not make him take it, you have hardly been a loving parent. Of course the child will love you that moment for being kind. Years later, if he's in braces, he will surely think you were unwise.

It's usually tough to be tough. Decent human beings don't enjoy the suffering of others. They identify so deeply with the victim that they want to bring relief as soon as possible. But that's exactly what allows them to be dominated as well. Millions of parents are doormats to their children. They feel sorry when the child cries because chores must be done. So Mother does the dishes while her three teen-age daughters watch the ideal American family on television.

Millions of married people are doormats to their mates. They feel so sorry for them when genuine frustrations occur. He's dog-tired from working and wants to stay home tonight. She's ready to swallow poison at not getting her way, so he gives in and drags himself to a party he can't stand. And that's the way it's been between them for all the years of their marriage. He knows he's dominated but feels powerless to do anything about it. He just can't stand others' being upset and takes it upon himself to put all right with the world even at the cost of denying himself repeatedly.

Other-pitiers, you're sweet and decent people but you're not all that helpful when you're too helpful.

WOMEN DO THE WASH, MEN CUT THE LAWN

One of the most powerful forces that makes us passive is the way our culture defines our roles. There is a pecking order among chickens. Rooster A can peck any other fowl in the barnyard. Rooster B can peck every fowl except A. And C can peck all those beneath him except A and B. And so it goes.

With people the pecking order is determined by several factors. For small children it's brute strength. In high school it may be based on popularity, good looks, sports ability, or grades. In the adult world it's usually power and money, but also one's sex.

Boys are taught that it's permissible to do certain kinds of work, such as carry out trash and mow lawns. Girls are trained to cook, wash dishes, and clean house. But it goes farther. For example, men are supposed to take charge, to lead, to make important decisions and women are expected to comply. Right there, in those two roles as defined by society, are the actual makings of a doormat. Society says certain people must play doormat to others and everybody goes along with the game. For instance, the poor usually humble themselves to the rich or famous, even when they are not under any direct influence of the wealthier one. Simply being poor places one in a category of people that are going to get rejected and ordered around.

Beethoven stepped out of his house one morning for a walk. He was wearing old clothes. He walked for a couple of hours and got lost. Not having money on him, he looked through the windows of homes and shops for help and was arrested as a vagabond. He naturally protested that he was the great Ludwig van Beethoven and should be released. (Notice how he too believed rank had its privileges.) Anyway, he was finally released the following day and the mayor had him driven home in the mayor's coach.

Had that happened to just any old, plain, and hungry vagabond, he probably would have been escorted out of town after spending a few more nights in jail. We are programmed to treat others in specific ways because of the roles we assign them. There was a time in this country when being an Irishman was as unacceptable to the establishment as it was to be a dog. Literally both were forbidden admission into some bars.

Today it's the Puerto Ricans, the blacks, and the Native Americans who are struggling for a place in the sun. Even today we find it hard for most of us to think of a woman in the White House. We are programmed to think of women as being followers, not leaders. That's programming, pure and simple.

Take heart, you losers! No matter how you were trained to think of yourself you can, *if you will question your training vigorously,* slowly develop a new philosophy. I recently spoke with a successful businessman who always felt sheepish in the company of men even slightly more successful than he. We talked about this for two sessions, after which he suddenly got the insight that he had been brainwashed to keep a low profile to his superiors. Now he realized he didn't need to do that another day of his life. That night he went to a social function where he was introduced to Mr. Big and was delighted to find how calmly he now took the whole affair.

IT'S MY NATURE

The surest way to become passive and to spend your life making everyone content at your expense is to believe it's your nature to be unassertive. Now how can anyone fight nature? If a man is born to be gentle and servile, how is he ever supposed to stand up, stick out his chest, and shout to the world, "I am somebody"?

Here is an example of a woman whom I was training to stand up for herself against her adolescent daughters. Betty wanted help with teaching them not to swear, especially at her when they did not get what they wanted. To tell them it was rude to curse their mother had no effect on them. What else could she do?

The girls, old enough to care for themselves, could be treated with a firm hand. I therefore instructed Betty to order them out of the home to live with relatives and friends if they were not going to respect her. She warned them of this intention and expected them to take her seriously. Within the week the oldest girl wanted something which Betty refused. The girl called her a couple of choice words. Betty was on the spot. Immediately she knew she had to do something tough or she'd never have the daughter's respect. They yelled at each other for a short while, but Betty ordered her out anyway. The girl stayed with her young adult friends. For several days Betty felt strong and gutsy. She was the classical marshmallow who suddenly got tough as a walnut. It thrilled her to be in charge of her family for once. Even the other children sensed a new strength in her and were tiptoeing around the house.

But the chicken in Betty started to wake up a few days later. Her guilt grew slowly until she felt like a wicked mother who could redeem herself only by making up with the girl and having her home again. The triumphant girl returned and walked all over mama like nothing ever happened. All Betty could say was, "I guess it's just my nature to be soft."

Nature? Hardly. At her age she was behaving with ninety-five percent programming and perhaps five percent nature. Maybe she wasn't as bold as her baby brother when they were in the crib, but that can hardly explain her timidity today, some forty years later.

Betty believed for so long that she simply could not stand to frustrate others that she seldom put herself to the test. If she had forced herself not to allow her daughter back home until the girl apologized, even if it took a month or two, Betty would soon have seen how perfectly capable she actually was at getting respect.

Just because you were trained to be fearful in your youth does not mean you cannot change later as an adult. You had better believe that you can change, or it will never happen.

I debated this point with Betty. I told her to stop believing that she could not change and she would see soon enough how she would change. She worked hard at trying to see herself as a strong person who was not ordained by God to bend to the will of everyone else. The next time her oldest girl sassed her rudely she was ordered out and she decided not to move back. But the other girls found a new respect for their mother and they stayed.

Another woman, Frances, thought she had to be a pushover to her daughter because she had always been one. I challenged this for her in the first interview. To see what is possible in therapy, study these fragments from her second session.

THERAPIST: Let's review the last session briefly.

CLIENT: When I came to you I was frustrated almost to the point of raging. I have a twenty-year-old daughter who is pregnant, unmarried, a former drug addict who left her child. She is divorced and is now pregnant again and living with me but not doing anything that I want her to do. She wouldn't change her bed linens, she was unclean, she wouldn't care for the dog, and didn't get up until one o'clock in the afternoon. She was cranky and hard to get along with, totally unhappy. You suggested that I had better get firm with her, close my purse, throw out the dog if I didn't want the dog and that I take her on *my* terms. And that's what I did.

T: In more detail, what happened then?

C: I went home after my interview and I told her where I had been. She was upset and she spent the next two days in her bedroom and didn't come out.

T: Did you tell her what the conditions were?

C: Oh, yes, I explained to her exactly what we talked about.

T: Okay.

C: As much as I could remember. In fact, when I left here I felt in a kind of euphoric state because I had gotten some kind of answer. So she spent two days in her bedroom and didn't come out for meals, didn't make any effort to communicate, and was very solemn and unhappy. And at the end of the second day, which was Sunday night, she came out of her bedroom cheerful, smiling, and I thought that was fine but we'll see how it goes. So I went to work Monday. When I came home from work Monday night there was a nice dinner waiting for me and the house was straightened up. We had barbecued chicken. And on Tuesday I had another nice dinner. And on Wednesday she had someplace to go, so she wrote me a note and she said: "Mother, there's a meat loaf in the refrigerator. All you have to do is put it in the oven. I'll be home later."

T: All this time you were doing all the cooking by yourself and for her too, even though she was sitting around the house polishing her nails or watching television?

C: Doing her handicraft work, right.

T: And she was a twenty-year-old woman?

C: We had a brief period after the first week or ten days or so when I had to get firm again.

T: What about that?

C: I just sat down and talked with her and I told her that either she acted her age and became a productive part of the family life or I'd kick her out.

T: Where would you kick her?

C: I don't know.

T: Would you do it?

C: No.

T: You wouldn't?

C: I wouldn't. But I told her I would.

T: That's not good enough. She may start testing you. If you say that you are going to get rid of her, that she had better cut the mustard if she wants to stay with you, then you had better be prepared to ship her off someplace if she doesn't. Don't threaten idly, it's not good. She is going to test you one of these days.

C: You're probably right.

T: Right now she is just a little bit scared, but she is going to start testing you more and more to see what you want. If you don't back it up and really hit her hard with it, she's going to realize that you have been bluffing and that you are not to be taken seriously.

C: Today I had a talk with her. We were just talking by

chance. It wasn't because I was coming here—I didn't even tell her I was coming back today. But we were talking about the child and all that, and she said this is the first time since she has been away from her child that she really has something to live for now and really do something with her life. And she is looking forward to the birth of the child, getting a job. She sounded very convincing and was smiling. She looked very nice, very neat and clean, and was in good humor. I don't know whether she just needed to have to be told that she finally had to buckle down or what. But whatever it is, it's been a really good relationship now. I can't believe it. It has turned absolutely 180 degrees. To have somebody come up naturally to you and smile and be the way you want them to be, seemingly happy.

T: Do you really think she is happy though?

C: Well, she seems to be. She has embroidered every little undershirt that she's bought for this baby. I haven't bought a thing. She's bought everything.

T: How does she intend to take care of this child after it's born?

C: I told her she could stay with me until she can get a job.

T: Who is going to take care of the baby?

C: She'll either have to have a baby-sitter come in or take it to a baby-sitter, because I work. She understands that she has to get up during the night and she's got to do the diapers and she's got to do the bottles, because I'm not going to be around.

T: Are you sure now?

C: I say so today but I suppose if the baby is lying there with dirty pants I would change it.

T: Of course. But that won't be a routine thing. Right?

C: Right.

T: You are not going to take these obligations off her back, are you?

C: No. After I talked with you, I got a better perspective on how a mother can get to be a total mother, even to the people you work with. I've been trying to notice whether I've been doing this at work also. And I have been.

T: Tell me more.

C: I just feel that I like to solve people's problems or something. So you listen to people and let them talk to you and sometimes you are worn out because you carry their problems rather than saying just forget it, or go handle it yourself. You're a big kid and that kind of thing. Anyway I'm happy that I came to you.

T: You have done very, very well, I must say.

C: When we talked the last time and you said kick her out, don't spend any money, and so on. I said: "Fine. This is really good. But I am now forty-three and I can't change my ways in one week."

T: I know.

C: And so I think it has to be a gradual sort of thing.

T: Certainly it'll be gradual. Don't overdo this business of asserting yourself. And of course by kicking her out I didn't mean that you put her bags on the sidewalk. That's ridiculous. Nobody is going to shove somebody out in the cold. If you're a monster, you do that, otherwise you don't. But you may want to start thinking now: "My daughter is really goofing off around here. I'm going to prove to her that I really mean business. What I might want to do is, I'll call up the welfare office and see whether they can't find a place for her."

C: This is what she is going to do this coming week. They won't talk with her yet, because she's due in December and if she has the paper work done in November, then after the baby is born she will qualify and that will carry her over until she can get a job. But the thing is she has to get a job, because living on welfare is not the answer either. Not for her and not for me.

T: But it would act as a temporary proof again that you mean what you say. She'll be out of the house and out alone, and she won't be starving or out on the streets either. That's not what we are interested in seeing.

C: She's a very talented girl, she's a very lovely girl. And she does beautiful handicraft work, and she has a whole lot going for her. That's why I was so concerned that I couldn't reach her. I didn't know how to get to her to get her motivated.

T: Okay, let's end at this point. I hope you continue doing as well as you are doing. I think it's great.

C: I think it's fantastic!

T: I agree.

4

The Moment of Truth

We are now at a point where talk can be converted into action. Thinking of what you'd like to do is about the easiest thing in the world, while doing it is about the toughest. There isn't anyone I know who hasn't behaved in a regrettable way and then spent days fantasizing how he or she might have changed things. Virtually all of us find it enormously difficult to do what our hearts and heads tell us to do. That's the moment of decision. It is a moment with which you **must** become thoroughly familiar so that you are not overwhelmed by it.

The moment you decide to assert yourself and to face one of those five coward makers you will experience a powerful temptation to back down. Your brain instantly urges you to escape, to rationalize, and to weasel your way out of a tight spot by any means you can. You may experience a moment of confusion, a fleeting panic so powerful that your best intentions shrivel like a leaf on fire.

That is the moment to be aware of. Try with all your might to be brave at the instant every feeling in your body compels you to be weak. Don't give in to that urge to be passive. Shout to yourself mentally: "Now, now, do it! Don't waver! Quickly, act, speak up, *stop being afraid.*"

If this vigorous self-talk fails to make you strong enough to assert yourself at the moment, don't despair. Keep up the self-talk. Rehearse what you wanted to say but did not say. Then, if you can face the moment of truth a few minutes later, do it then. Even if it takes hours or days to get up courage to make your confrontation, do it *whenever you can.* It may not change a situation if you assert yourself late in the game. At this point you need practice more than success. It is more important to do than to do well (see my book on self-discipline: *How to Do What You Want to Do*).

The day will come when you will delay less and less before you speak up. However, at first you may take quite a while getting to it.

This moment is often so scary, so filled with anticipated guilt and embarrassment, that it stops strong and intelligent persons dead in their tracks. It stops psychologists, psychiatrists, politicians, and actors—people who are usually comfortable with others. Even they can talk themselves into the best of intentions and then chicken out at the last moment.

Therefore, to help you bridge the distance between daydreaming and action, study the many examples of self-assertion I have dealt with in my own practice. Each of the following examples depicts real persons, but identifying information has been altered in order to protect the identity of the client.

First, carefully read each example of a person finally saying and doing what he or she meant to say or do. Then put yourself in that person's role and do the best you can in it. If you manage most of these examples, you will have done a fantastic job of teaching yourself to stand up for yourself.

STANDING UP TO CHILDREN

Those who are truly afraid to assert themselves, even in normal ways, should start with children. Then later, when they have their courage up in controlling misbehaving children, they can be promoted to the tougher relationships with adults.

When the children were cutting across her lawn on the way to school Mildred wanted to tell them to use the sidewalk but wouldn't bring herself to do it. She feared a fifth-grader would sass her back or make a gesture to which she would have been too startled to respond. That would have humiliated her, or so she thought.

Mildred was encouraged to recognize how she was talking herself into feeling like a fool. What if a fresh kid talked back to her? I asked her to imagine precisely how bad that would really be. First, the neighbors probably wouldn't even see the event. Secondly, if they did, she could simply complain to them about the rude behavior of children these days and get total agreement. Thirdly, if she spoke in a friendly manner, the children would probably respond in like manner. Fourthly, even if a boy was obscene, that's his problem, not hers. Why should she act as though she did something wrong? And lastly, since when do names and gestures hurt, anyway?

You may ask, "Am I expected seriously to go through a whole lot of mental analysis each time I am confronted with a decision to act?"

Yes, I'm afraid so. Why should that surprise you? You

are already doing mental analyzing when you talk yourself into behaving cowardly. Use mental challenging to change those fearful thoughts into strong assertive thoughts. The only way that can be done is by thinking rationally.

DISSATISFACTION AT THE RESTAURANT

Who hasn't been served a bad meal? When this happened to you did you just choke it down? Or did you protest? The mature person may not expect a whole meal to be served to replace an unacceptable item, but he does owe it to the restaurant to let his complaint be known.

"But why isn't it just easier," Ellie said, "to leave your plate and not return to the place again?"

"Because you avoid growing up by not facing tough problems, and you don't correct the fault with the restaurant," I pointed out.

"Who cares?" she replied smartly.

"I would think you would. What will happen to you if you don't reject bad food?"

"I'll just get up and leave, that's all."

"And could that get to be a habit?"

"I suppose so. But I just can't stand to embarrass the waitress or to make a scene to the management."

"Who says you can embarrass the waitress or that you necessarily will have a scene with the manager?"

Ellie replied, "I've seen some young waitresses dissolve into tears when someone complained about the food."

I asked, "You mean a person called the girl over and told her very warmly and with a smile that the soup was cold and would she please bring a bowl of hot soup?"

"No, he didn't do it that way. He told her he had always had trouble with that particular chain of restaurants, that it was the second worst restaurant in the world, and that he could not quite remember the name of the first one."

"In other words, the fellow was rude and thoughtless."

"Right."

"So who says you have to be that way too? As an exercise, I want you to eat out several times before I see you again and complain nicely to the waiter or waitress about anything that makes you unhappy. Is the bread too stale, the crackers not crisp, the knife too dull? Then make a gentle fuss about it and report back to me how you felt."

Ellie soon had an opportunity to try her self-assertion skills. But she did badly. The breaded shrimp broke under her bite like hard crackers. She drank her glass of water and didn't get a refill. And when the manager came by later and asked if everything was all right, she said, "Everything was fine."

"How did you talk yourself into such cowardice, Ellie? Do you remember your thoughts?" I inquired.

"I sure do. I know I was wrong but I couldn't seem to do anything about it. I said I didn't want to make a fuss and have them think I was a difficult person. I guess I want people to like me so much I won't defend myself."

"That's not entirely it, Ellie. The real reason you didn't complain was that you thought that being disliked by them was awful and could upset you. The first thought, that they might not like you, was actually correct. The second thought, that it would hurt to be rejected, that doesn't make sense."

Rejection is only sad, not the end of the world. And rejection by people you hardly know is even less threatening. With practice, Ellie learned to order a proper meal and once she even turned back two steaks and was about to do so to a third when her better judgment told her the place just didn't have good ones.

LITTLE COMPLAINTS PROVIDE EXCELLENT PRACTICE

Changing your personality from being a pushover to being self-interested requires practice. Do not let little opportunities pass or you will suffer for it. Practice makes the master whether we are talking about dancing, yodeling, or giving orders. Therefore, when you get the chance to correct an irritation, do it nicely if you can. But most importantly, do it. If it can't be done with polish at first, keep it up until you become suave in registering complaints. That's an art, one of the neatest to acquire. A person who is a master at this possesses several traits: self-confidence (derived through trial and error); calmness (because situations are not allowed to get out of hand); and popularity (because people look up to those who have good feelings about themselves).

Recently I had a minor opportunity to practice my own self-assertion skills. Being in a rush and having only a half hour for dinner, I called a restaurant to reserve a table and told them I would be there at 6 P.M.

I placed the order over the phone because the restaurant did a carry-out business as well and was quite accustomed to this procedure. When I got there I had the reserved table all right, but the dish was not served until 6:15 P.M.

This annoyed me because of the time pressure I was under. I had deliberately called in ahead of time to avoid precisely this situation. My first impulse was to let the matter ride and to see the problem from the restaurant's point of view. Perhaps the management didn't want to put food on the table until I was there because it could get cold if I were a few minutes late. Maybe it had been cheated before by accepting orders over the phone and then not having them picked up. But the more I realized that I was backing away from a confrontation, however small, the more annoyed I became with myself. So I did what I always advise others to do: challenge the nonsense I was talking myself into. This was quickly accomplished and suddenly I had no qualms about going to the waitress and instructing her as follows:

"I called to have my food ready by 6 P.M. because I want to be somewhere else shortly. Hereafter, please serve my food at that time whether I'm here or not. If the food gets cold, that's my problem. If I don't show up, bill me (the waitress knew me and where I worked). I'll take full responsibility for what happens if you do as I ask. Is that all right with you?"

I haven't had a chance to try that situation again. However, if I get the same waitress, I'll only have to remind her of our previous conversation. If I get another waitress, I'll know that I had better caution her of these conditions. I'm glad I did it, not because it was such a big issue (it wasn't) but because I did have a slight hesitancy about talking up and I overcame it. I was able to do that because I have faced such situations countless times before and each one made the next one easier. That makes my life easier because it's less frustrating.

Practice asserting yourself on minor issues, not just major ones. Don't try to lift a hundred pounds until you've comfortably lifted ten.

WHAT DIFFERENCE CAN I MAKE?

Try to talk yourself out of the belief that your confrontations won't make any difference in the long run. Yours is only one voice, you think, so how can you have any clout anyway?

That's a serious mistake. It repeatedly amazes me how much social force can be set in motion by very few complaints. I've always been impressed by the story of a gentleman who was expecting a political appointment in Washington and had the full support of his senator. As the date of his appointment neared, the senator called to tell his friend of his need to go back on his support for the appointment.

"But why, senator?" he asked.

"Because I've received enough mail complaining of your appointment that I think it would go against public sentiment at this time."

"Mail, how much mail?"

The senator pulled out a couple dozen letters as his total evidence of the man's unpopularity. The senator stuck to his guns. That handful of letters made a big difference in that man's life. When you think of writing your congressman or of making a complaint that strikes you as being puny in comparison to the persons or organization you are confronting, think of this example.

A Boy Scout at summer camp was to receive lifesaving instructions from a fellow we shall call Mike. The instructor knew his business well enough but he didn't understand or care about the feelings of the Scouts he instructed. When Tommy didn't catch on, Mike used profanity in correcting him and did it before the whole class.

Tommy told his dad about this treatment on the last day of camp, whereupon the father related this to the camp director. The father was told that such behavior by an instructor is not allowed and that Mike would have been called on the carpet or fired if the director had been told of the problem earlier. However, since he could no longer do anything about the situation on the last day of camp, he would surely not hire Mike again for the coming season.

That's what the complaint of one little Boy Scout achieved. You make more of a difference than you realize. Try it and see. Even if you aren't always sure of the effect you'll have, try it anyway. That's what Dan did when he called the tennis club to reserve a court but found the phone busy every time he dialed.

Finally he made contact with the girl at the desk, reserved a court, and was about to hang up when he remembered the homework assignments I had given him about speaking up about things that troubled him. So he proceeded.

"Say, is there something wrong with your phone? I got a busy signal for the past fifteen minutes. Is someone using your phones who has no business tying up your lines?" Dan asked.

"You say you tried calling us for the past fifteen minutes but got a busy signal?"

"Yes. I must have dialed your number five or six times and got a busy signal each time."

"That's funny. The phone has been open except for one call I took awhile ago."

So be it. Anyway the seed was planted. If the girl was guilty of tying up the phone, she'll think twice before doing this again.

Don't curse the darkness, light a candle instead.

FIFTY MILLION FRENCHMEN *CAN* BE WRONG

He was an elderly man in a small town some fifty years ago when long beards were out of style. For some reason Henry wanted a long beard and all the teasing or rejection in the world wasn't going to get him to cut it off. Even when the kids ran alongside of him, jeering over his beard, he did not give in and remove it. He went to his grave, proud, undaunted, and doing his own thing to the very end. I admire him for it.

If doing your own thing doesn't hurt anyone else, what right have others to make you stop? None, I say. And that frees me and you from living through the eyes, thoughts, and tastes of others. To assert yourself in situations like this, you had better figure that you're right and everyone else is wrong. Fifty million Frenchmen *can* be wrong, contrary to the old saying.

A friend of mine never sent Christmas cards to persons he saw over the holidays. He couldn't understand why he needed to send a card to his neighbor when they saw each other practically every day and to whom he wished a "Merry Christmas" in person. His wife was always uneasy receiving cards from friends all over town knowing that they would not be returning the favor. But he stuck to his guns even though he got pressure from his wife and was teased by his friends.

Another fellow I met used to melt a pat or two of butter in his coffee despite the stares and jokes of his dinner companions. It wasn't hurting anyone else even if it may not have been the best dietary habit for him. I shudder to think what his blood vessels looked like. But that was his problem. He liked butter in his coffee and wouldn't let the pressure of his companions change his preference.

Tony came from Europe. He had a small business in a town out west and dreamed someday of making lots of money. For years he was careful to save his money, knowing the day would come when he'd need a cash down payment for a deal he couldn't refuse. All through World War II he kept his eyes open and waited for the right opportunity. It finally came. Tony decided to buy some cornfields south of town and convert them slowly into a housing development.

The businessmen had a good chuckle over this move. They thought he was super optimistic and would lose his shirt. Then the housing market took off after the war and returning veterans needed places to live. Tony's housing addition wasn't much at first. He sold a few lots to a builder who put up a couple of buildings which made a handsome profit. Then Tony realized that he made enough profit from the sale of his lots that he could build his own houses and sell them for a handsome profit too. It was the beginning of a large development in that western town that made Tony one of the richest and most respected men in the area.

He took a risk and proved he could be right and all the experts could be wrong. Majority opinion is not always proof of wisdom. Right is right whether that belief is held by one person or a million. Don't be afraid the next time you take a new direction all by yourself. Thoreau suggests you might be listening to a different drummer. Even more to the point, however, *you might be the only one marching to the right beat.* It happens all the time that one person is right and the whole world is wrong. Remember the Wright brothers? Or Einstein? And how about Columbus?

STATE THE LOGICAL CONSEQUENCES

Beth was having serious problems with her seventeen-year-old daughter, Marge. The girl would not clean her room, pick up her clothes, come in at a decent hour, or get up early enough to arrive at her job on time. Beth handled this problem in the most common way. She nagged the girl constantly. She'd tell her to pick up her clothes and put them in the hamper. Mother was not a maid. Mother had many other things to do and the least the daughter could do was to spare her the indignity of picking up after her as though Mother were her personal servant.

On and on she'd go in this fashion, complaining about this or that until the girl would get so fed up with being picked on that she once attacked her mother so savagely the woman had to be hospitalized.

Obviously this sweet and caring mother was nice to a fault. She lost complete control of her daughter because she failed to take one very important step. The mother never told Marge what would happen if she did not do as Mother commanded. All Marge got was a lot of words, not a promise of painful consequences. Since

Marge did not know what would happen to her for not getting to her job on time, she had little to fear. It is only when you show people what will happen rather than predict what will happen that they have reason to listen and change their behavior.

For example, Marge began coming around very nicely when Beth refused to wake her up for her summer job. When the girl lost that job after oversleeping three times she fully realized that *(a)* she could no longer count on her mother and *(b)* she'd have to get herself out of the sack if she wanted a job and spending money.

Notice, Beth didn't warn her daughter she was not going to wake her up. That would only have been more talk. Beth got quick results only when she didn't wake her up. It was the action, *not* the talk about an action, that got results.

Before she would put pressure on her daughter, however, Beth was told what to expect. First, things get worse. Marge screamed, became vulgar, and cursed her mother viciously for not waking her up. But Beth walked away each time. Second, Marge leaped on her mother and began striking her. This time Beth swung back. Finally, Beth informed the girl in no uncertain terms that she would no longer wake her up or pick up her dirty clothes, and that was that. If Marge wanted the freedom of an adult, then she would be required to be responsible for her own actions.

Sounds simple, doesn't it? Yet, as often as I've stated what the consequences will be for certain acts, there are always some persons who miss the point. Recently a woman complained about her husband's unpleasantness at the dinner table. He corrected the children endlessly.

"What can I do?" she asked. "I've told him a million times I don't want shouting matches when we're eating."

"Why don't you just take your plate and go to the living room. Tell him you won't join him for dinner again until he stops his arguing."

Chances are this advice will work very well. Try acting instead of talking for a change!

SAY "NO" ON PURPOSE

If you're going to be master of your world, you had better learn how to say, "No." After you practice awhile, use that skill in situations when you think it's appropriate. In fact, when you could go either way, try saying no once in a while just for practice.

Sounds strange, uncharitable, selfish? Perhaps. But if such an exercise actually makes you a stronger person, then it can't be all bad. Building up your self-esteem and confidence are worthy goals even if you are hard-nosed sometimes.

Take the case of the female in our society today and the effects the sexual revolution has had on her. It is now reasoned that women, because they are equal to men and because pregnancy is so easily controlled, don't have to be so touchy about their sex lives. They can carry on like men have been doing for a long time. So why would a woman not want to take advantage of this freedom?

Some women, however, feel that this greater freedom is not a freedom at all. Most men now expect them to say yes because there is little reason to say no. That subtle pressure is actually a loss of freedom and it puts them back where they were before the sexual revolution. Then a woman was told to say no, now she's told to say yes. So who is free? Who is in charge?

Women will not be liberated until they take the option themselves to say yes or no. To learn that habit, they have the right and the obligation to practice saying no sometimes when a yes is expected. Lucy did this one night after a date. Her escort had shown her a good time and she enjoyed his company. In front of her door, however, she had to decide whether or not to let him in. A twinge of guilt touched her conscience when she thought of how he was expecting more attention and when she thought of how disappointed he would be if rejected especially after he had been so expectant and spent so much money on her.

Normally Lucy would have asked him in and disliked herself for it in the morning, not because she satisfied him but because she didn't satisfy herself. When she let the feelings of others dictate her behavior, she didn't like herself.

On this particular night Lucy really wanted to spend more time with her date, but she didn't like the pity she felt for him. It would have been immediately easier on her to say yes, but, to develop her assertiveness, she forced herself to say no. There was a good-night kiss and away he went. She was naturally uncomfortable as she thought over the evening, but in the end she felt a sense of satisfaction that she risked rejection and showed courage. After that the next assertive act was slightly easier. And that's the way it went until she could stand up for herself with ease. It took a couple of years of this sort of forcing herself at times to say no when the issue was about evenly balanced before she was well trained to do so habitually.

If someone asks to borrow money from you and you feel so-so about it, refuse the favor half the time at least, simply because you get valuable practice in saying no. The same can be done when you are asked to baby-sit, lend your car, your tools, or your clothes, run errands, go to this show or that show.

Don't practice saying no when the issue is important. That would be clearly self-defeating. If you're dying to buy a house and your family is all in favor of it, that's no time to practice being negative. Or, if someone asks you for a favor that is fair and important to that person, the decent thing to do is to give in when you can. That is, after all, one of the ingredients in human affairs that makes life pleasant and builds friendships. But, not all decisions are better because they please others. What about you? Practice doing your own thing but only when it makes sense.

TAKE A RISK

When you come right down to it, all assertiveness is risk-taking. The moment you get stepped on and you want to stop the abuse, you risk being abused, fired from your job, or rejected by someone you love. Something serious can usually happen when you deny others what is or seems to be important to them. That's precisely why saying and doing what you mean is among the most difficult tasks in the world. Acting upon your convictions is the most difficult of all human efforts.

If you want to learn to assert yourself, learn to take

a risk. That's easily said. But I can assure you from twenty-five years of experience as a clinical psychologist that it tries men's souls, makes women weep, and brings giants to their knees. Try some of these actions if they seem appropriate to your life. Don't just think about them, do them.

1. Ask for a raise if you think you have one coming. Have another job ready that you can accept before you make this move. Then tell your boss you have a better offer and will leave if you aren't given a raise. Don't just think about doing this another day. Do it, now. Take the risk and either get your raise or get a better job.

2. Refuse to cooperate with abuse, even if it endangers your marriage. When Jerry wouldn't pick up his beer cans around the house even though Mabel often asked him, and even though she often picked up after him, Mabel decided she had had enough. She determined simply to refuse to pick up another can even if the cans eventually piled to the ceiling and even if Jerry got terribly angry over it. In this case Mabel got results after stepping over beer cans for three weeks. Terry didn't explode, as she had feared, he just got annoyed a few times when he realized she wasn't cleaning up after him. She took a risk and won her case, and did she ever feel good afterward!

3. Penalize an immature reaction to a penalty. This can be particularly sticky because feelings often run high when you penalize someone. Watch out when you frustrate a person a second time for not accepting the first penalty.

Morris wouldn't agree to buy a new car that Delores felt she needed or she'd "die." During an argument she wanted to make it clear how angry and hurt she was, so she smashed her whole set of dishes on the kitchen floor. She expected Morris to take pity on her and at least clean them up even if he wouldn't get her the car, but he didn't. Breaking the dishes was another immature antic that required affirmative action also. So the kitchen stayed a mess for days while she refused to clean it up or cook. He took the kids out to eat and endured nights alone in bed. The marriage reached a dangerous point of separation, but he didn't give in. When all tempers cooled, the kitchen was cleaned and he had won new respect from his wife. She never tried that stunt again.

4. Be daring. Break the rules and make a few of your own. Do you know how Aristotle Onassis got started on his fortune? He stood outside an important person's office every day for three weeks until he was asked in. The secretary told him it was no use, he'd never get in to see the executive. But Onassis was determined. He took the risk of looking like a fool, took the risk of being thrown out bodily, and stood his ground. His reward was a life of wealth and power.

Psychological slaves have chains on their brains, not on their legs. You break them by risking more pain. The risk is often worth the gain.

FRANK TALK IN BED

One of the most important occasions that calls for expressing yourself according to your tastes is in bed. Far too many people are unhappy with their sex lives because they don't assert themselves in the matter of making love. Perhaps you're afraid your mate will think you're crude if you describe how you want to be fondled. Don't be. If you don't tell her, she can't possibly read your mind. And if she gets shocked at your suggestion, that's her problem. The worst that can happen is that she will refuse you.

If you have a favorite position, request it from time to time. You're supposed to enjoy sex, remember? Unless you make your wishes known and press for them a good percentage of the time, you're not likely to enjoy your love life. Some men like using sexy language during lovemaking, others want the light on during the entire episode. Some want to draw it out, others to reach climax quickly. Whatever makes you happy in bed and doesn't cause pain to your partner is a fair request and has a right to be asked for some of the time. And if you truly want a happy sex life, you had better see to it that those important practices are expressed once in a while until you can honestly say that you are reasonably content.

It is the female, however, who is usually the least satisfied partner. She has been carrying on her sex life for centuries not fully knowing what makes her satisfied or not daring to ask. Or if she does ask and her mate does not understand her request or convinces her she's weird, she gives up her goals and settles for sex his way.

Many women do not find intercourse itself all that great. It can drive some of them wild, but the vast majority of women cannot even come to orgasm through intercourse, much less prefer it. If women were to press for their style of lovemaking, it would go something like this.

There would be lots of touching, feeling, kissing, hugging, and bodily contact, not just genital contact. This, for many women, could go on a while, during which time there would be soft love talk and laughter.

There would be absolutely no rush. Instead of a brief encounter which takes most males from start to finish no more than five to twenty minutes, these women want their love to be drawn out, to increase slowly until they gradually become more and more excited. Then when they reach a peak they want to be let down a bit so the whole process can be built up again.

If the male is finished at that point, she doesn't want him hopping out of bed or rolling over to sleep. She is just getting started. Many women are perfectly capable of a mysterious gift called multiple orgasms. That means they can release sexual energy three, four, or half a dozen times at a setting. And whether the man is through or not, she usually is not.

DON'T WAIT FOR THE PERFECT TIME
OR THE PERFECT SOLUTION

You will seldom achieve full stature as a mature adult if you wait for conditions to be perfect before asserting yourself. Yet this is a most common rationalization for not acting in your own best interests.

I once received a phone call from a man who complained of his impossible wife. It seems she had torn up her garden in a state of great anger. He had tried being reasonable numerous times before, but when she became frustrated she acted like an angry child. What could he do about the marriage? he wondered.

I told him over the phone to come in for counseling with her so we could understand why the two of them were having such serious problems. It was clear to me by then that she was acting as she did because she knew he would tolerate it.

His first response to my suggestion was to tell me to hold the phone while he went into the next room to ask if she'd agree to come. Can you imagine that? This fellow was disgusted with his wife, wasn't sure he wanted to live in the same house, and still thought he ought to ask her if she wanted to get help.

"Don't ask her," I urged. "Tell her, or there will be serious consequences if she doesn't."

"But this may not be a good time to put such pressure on her," he protested.

"True, but if you wait for ideal conditions before you act, people are going to manipulate you over and over again. Now go to your wife and tell her you've made an appointment for counseling and if she cares about the marriage, she'll accept. If not, you'll be considering drastic action."

"Well, I don't know. Suppose it doesn't work. I don't want to divorce her after all. Wouldn't it be better to talk this over with her again until I can see for sure that I'm making the right move?"

And so it went until it was clear he was not ready for action, and might never be. There are some times when it is better to act than not to act. However, since we can't be sure which time is best, we are better off taking our chances rather than waiting for a perfect time.

This same fellow once had a quarrel with his wife while they were driving to a party. She became angry over something and insisted that he turn the car around or she'd walk home. There it was again, D Day (Decision Day). Was this the right time to teach her not to lose control? Was it really wisest to stop the car, let her out as she demanded, and proceed to the party without her?

Who knows? If it's not snowing and she's not seventy-five miles from home, maybe now would be as good a time as any. Or maybe such an act would push her into a divorce court.

These are difficult decisions at best. Still I would urge that more often than not a decision to act, even if you cannot be certain of its outcome, is better than no decision at all. Sitting on the fence of indecision only gives you a sore rear. Far better to use your best judgment, play the percentages, and do something increasingly daring when less forceful methods have proved to be ineffective.

There is no right and precise solution to our problems, so don't hold off deciding for that brilliant moment when you will absolutely and certainly know what to do.

TEST YOUR BELIEFS

When you encounter a problem that calls for an examination of an old belief, don't be surprised if you find that so difficult that you would rather give in than change your philosophy. Let me cite three examples of persons who successfully changed their deepest beliefs when their reason suggested they were right to do so and who profited greatly by so doing.

Hal's adolescent daughter came home late one night with liquor on her breath. She was only fourteen and this development shocked him and his wife. What were they to do? The usual lecture and grounding as a penalty followed, but they both felt this was insufficient to make a firm impression. They had a conference and both hit on the same idea: call the parents of her friends, call the police, and finally place charges against an older girl (the driver) for contributing to the delinquency of minors.

Now came the dilemma. Do you squeal on your daughter's friends? Do you in fact squeal on your own child? She could wind up in the police station if they did. Nevertheless they gulped hard a few times and phoned the parents and the police and blew the lid off the whole episode. There was a distressing time for some weeks, but the daughter and her friends were sufficiently sobered not to be tempted to suffer such a swift penalty again.

The second example is of Monty, a fine young man with high ambitions who was going steady with Pauline. It was her desire to get married and have a family rather than go to college. His plans were the reverse. His head told him to break off with the girl and make school his first priority, but his ethical principles told him it was wrong to discard someone simply because she didn't fit perfectly into his plans. He would have felt quite guilty over hurting her feelings by rejecting her.

The longer Monty thought things over and the more he learned about human behavior, the more courage he got to defy his earlier teachings. He became convinced that Pauline would survive the disappointment and that he would not be directly responsible for her disturbance. People disturb themselves in the final analysis, so why accept blame for what she was doing to herself?

Then he realized that he could not be happy with Pauline if he did not get his education first. He counted too, so why shouldn't he look out for his welfare as well as hers? If their love had depth, it would survive the years while he would be in school. If it didn't, now was the time to find that out.

And that's what happened. She couldn't wait and therefore married someone else after he was in school two years. He earned his degree and married happily a few years later.

My third example concerns a woman who was always taught that it was monstrously rude not to cater to guests in every way. As a result she had a half dozen guests in the home practically every day and she couldn't get rid of the company until about ten thirty or eleven at night. On top of all this, her phone would ring constantly and friends would take hours of her time chatting, keeping her from her duties.

One day her frustrations and her highly prized principles hit the fan. She had had enough and began saying so and meaning it. It wasn't always done with the greatest tact, but it was done nevertheless. What she lost in social activity she gained in peace and quiet and she felt great about standing up for herself.

WRITE OUT YOUR PROGRAM FOR CHANGE

A father once told me of the great difficulty he was having making his daughter mind him. She was a bright girl but very headstrong. His wife had died a year before and it was all he could do to stay ahead of his strong-willed child.

I analyzed his problem in this way. His daughter was unmanageable because he simply did not do two things that would have made him an effective father. First, he did not make it clear to his child what he routinely expected of her. He would preach endlessly when she misbehaved, but this only bored her. Secondly, he didn't tell her what the consequence would be if she came home late, didn't do her chores, etc.

We decided he might be more effective if he wrote out his expectations along with a list of the penalties. That way there would be no misunderstanding of what he wanted and what would happen if his rules were ignored.

He came in at his next visit with the following list, wondering if he had done well and wisely.

CHORES

Monday	Put away laundry
Tuesday	Bring in trash cans
Wednesday	Clean yard
Thursday	Sweep porch
Friday	Weed garden
Saturday	Sweep garage

ACTION	CONSEQUENCE
Late to meals	Miss the meal
Disobey orders	No television
Neglect dog	Lose dog
Messy room	Sleep in bedroll
Late to school	No play after school
Neglect chores	No allowance
Eat junk foods	No treats

When I saw the girl after she was handed this piece of good news she was so angry she could hardly talk.

"Why did you tell my dad to write up this paper? He's

got me working every day. And if I don't do right, he's going to really clobber me. I don't have any freedom any more at all. I wish my mother were back."

We can all understand her frustration. She had never dealt with such firmness before and it scared and angered her. Nevertheless she required a structured home where she knew what to expect. Her father wasn't sure he was doing right, but I assured him he was on the right track. His expectations weren't unreasonable. He put them on paper so there could be no dispute over what he wanted and what she could expect. And if he backed up with action what he said he would do, there was every reason to believe he'd be more assertive over his daughter.

In the past he was often angry with her. He'd scold and even smack her on occasion. It did little good. His aggression wasn't what she needed, only his firmness. And it's the former she was getting.

Though she fought against this setup for about a solid month, the relationship gradually improved. It meant a lot of fights between father and daughter, but in the end his assertiveness as outlined on his paper began to take hold. She hated him when she couldn't manipulate him, but in short order she learned that if she was late to dinner she just missed out. That was all.

She fought like a wildcat but had to give in finally and learned a new respect for her father.

THE JUST REASONABLY CONTENT

What is the JRC? It is a term I have coined to express the point to which you had better strive if you want your relationship to thrive, the point where you can say, "Now I'm *just* *r*easonably *c*ontent."

Any relationship can survive fairly well if both parties are at the JRC. Both may want more benefits and favors from the arrangement and can continue to work at making themselves happier. However, the marriage, the friendship, or the job will be in good balance when each is just reasonably content.

You may feel selfish and guilty for wanting to please yourself. You've been taught all your life that love thrives only when you deny yourself and when you continually go out of your way to please the other person.

Up to a point this is true. Your spouse, boss, or friend is not going to feel very loving toward you if you never satisfy his or her wants. Your obligation in any partnership is to consider what's important to the other person and please that person. But how much? In the past we have believed it was wise to please until it hurt. The more you did for someone, the more you would be loved.

Wrong. You have the obligation to please your partner until he or she is at the JRC. Then it's his or her obligation to bring you to the same point. If you two follow this idea, you'll actually be pleasing each other most of the time, and at approximately the same time.

The best way to assure yourself of happiness in any relationship is to be concerned about your own interests and to please yourself as well as your partner. Do you honestly believe others will look out for your interests if you don't? Perhaps a rare soul will, but most of us are not saints.

To repair your relationship you may want to get more

respect from your partner first, and this in turn may lead to love and affection. And the way to get respect is to show the partner that your needs and desires are important and had better be taken into account. In fact, your needs and desires are every bit as important as the partner's. You're not demanding more satisfaction, nor will you tolerate less *as a rule.* At any one time you may be unhappier than your partner. That's the only way it could be. When you are *chronically* dissatisfied, however, at the price of pleasing your mate, neighbor, or colleague, then you have not only the right but the *obligation* to protect yourself. Your partner's respect for you is at stake, and the very relationship itself. Stand up for yourself as much and for whatever length of time it takes until you feel you are *just reasonably content.*

Things may get much worse before you reach that goal. No one likes to change, especially when it means sacrifice. That makes no difference. If you don't stick up for your welfare now, you'll only suffer a while longer until you finally do reach for the JRC, or fear doing so and get sick, or give up and get out.

5

The JRC in Action

Hubert doesn't realize it yet but he is beginning to lose his love for his wife. She gets her way so often at his expense that he's getting *(a)* to dislike himself for being so weak, *(b)* to dislike her for insisting on having her way practically all the time, and *(c)* to dislike the marriage because it has become a load he is not happy to carry.

"What do you want most from your wife? What must she do to make you happy?" I asked.

"I'd jump for joy if she would show a little eagerness for one of my suggestions. She's always finding holes in everything I suggest. I suggest a trip, she thinks we could get hurt. I think we ought to paint the house, but she thinks it'll cost too much. There's something wrong with almost every idea I have."

"So what happens?"

"So we don't take the trip or paint the house, or give the party, or do anything. We just sit and watch television. Saturday night movie for her is the television movie. We even have popcorn during the movies. How does that strike you?"

"What would happen if you went on a trip, painted

the house, or went to a movie, each time by yourself if she gave you static first?"

"She'd insist I was being selfish and didn't care about her. She'd insist I was only thinking of myself and that a marriage is supposed to be a fifty-fifty deal."

"She's right. Marriages work much better if each party is reasonably satisfied. Why don't you just go ahead and do what would make you happier?" I urged him.

"Because it would endanger my marriage. I love my wife and don't want to see anything happen to my marriage."

"Then, if you truly believe that, you had better make yourself more content, or there may not be a marriage someday. Don't you see that unless you force her to give in to you until you are just reasonably content, your marriage doesn't stand a chance of being happy for long?"

"But then what happens to her if I get my way at her expense?"

"She becomes less happy. But don't worry. She's got too much contentment right now at your expense. I'll bet she's fairly content with things as they are, isn't she?"

"You can say that again. She told me the other day she had things exactly as she wanted them."

"See what I mean? She's been busy making herself happy, and I respect her for it. What she doesn't understand is that both of you had better be at the JRC most of the time for the marriage to work. Therefore, pressure her into changing, whether she likes it or not, and keep it up until you've reached a point where you can feel just reasonably content."

"What happens then?"

"Then you have an obligation to ask how she feels about the benefits you're getting. Is she reasonably content too when you're just reasonably content? If so, you've got it made. If not, she may need more time to understand your goals, or you may want to decide for a divorce or separation."

"Is that my only option?"

"You have four choices: *(a)* Make yourself reasonably content at the cost of temporarily frustrating her, *(b)* give up the struggle and stop expecting your way, *(c)* let her become happy while you become sick and miserable, or *(d)* fight for your happiness with a possible divorce as the outcome. It's been my experience that standing up for your rights against all odds is one of the best ways to save most relationships."

"I'll try it. It just might improve things," he said with eagerness.

"That's right," I agreed. "It just might improve things."

AM I BEING FAIR?

A female client was having difficulty with her children because she was inadequate. She had difficulty asserting herself only when her children would throw back the accusation that she was not being fair in her treatment of them. This accusation easily evoked a feeling of guilt, which she found hard to combat. She honestly wanted to be a fair person and not to favor one child over another. The merest suggestion that maybe she was doing precisely that would immobilize her. She asked what she could do about this, if anything.

I pointed out to her that the next time she was accused of being unfair she should give it some thought, but not more than a few minutes. If she could agree that her child was being treated unfairly, she had the moral obligation to change her own behavior. If, however, at that time she was still not sure she had been unfair, then I instructed her to go ahead as she initially expected and not to worry about whether she was fair or not. I urged her to consider the following:

She could never be completely sure whether she was totally fair or not no matter how hard she tried. The best she could do was to give it a reasonable examination and then act. Sometimes it is simply more important to do something than it is to be absolutely certain that you are doing something right.

Secondly, by setting rules that might be unfair, she would at least get some feedback from that action. If she did not do this, she could in no way learn whether or not she was in fact being unfair. You sometimes have to go through with your plans and see what the results are before you know whether you are being decent and equitable.

And lastly, I pointed out that letting a child experience some unfairness is hardly the end of the world. As a matter of fact, it is frequently an important aspect of a child's growing up. This is an unfair world and any child who is raised in it without being exposed to unfairness is going to have a hard time indeed. What would happen if you raised your child with one hundred percent fairness, and he or she was totally unexposed to the meanness, the pettiness, and the greediness of other people? What do you think that person is going to encounter away from home? I can tell you with great certainty. That person will be completely disillusioned, depressed, and will develop all kinds of fears about a world that is inconsiderate of children's feelings.

It takes time to get used to almost any condition whether it be poverty, wealth, warm weather, cold weather, pleasant treatment, mean treatment, or what have you. Any child growing up in this world is going to be exposed to unfairness. Why be overly concerned about those times when you are not really sure whether you are being just or not? By all means try to be fair, but a little unkindness is hardly going to be a disaster, since the child may learn to cope with it. There will be more inconsiderateness from the persons he encounters later in life.

LISTEN WITH YOUR EYES

Gus was a heavy sleeper. This annoyed Nattie more and more, because she had to pester him each morning to get him off to work on time. He'd storm at her because she let him oversleep and she'd yell back that she had called him fifteen minutes ago and he had answered that he was awake. How was she to know he went back to sleep?

And so it went, day after day. And she was tired of it. "What can I do?" she asked in some desperation. "How can I make a grown man get up in the morning if he doesn't want to?"

"By telling him in a different way," I responded.

"What do you mean?"

"I mean you have been *telling* him to get up. You naturally thought he did most of his listening through his ears."

Nattie laughed at this despite the fact that she was in an angry mood. "You mean he *doesn't* listen through his ears? Have I been wrong all these years?" she laughed.

"Yes, in a manner of speaking you have been wrong. Why else would you be here talking to me? Something has to be wrong with your psychology or you wouldn't be having this problem in the first place. Gus and a great many people listen to what they see, not to what they hear. They believe their eyes, not their ears. Therefore, change your approach in the morning. Tell him tonight you'll call him once when it's time for him to get up. If he doesn't get up, he'll oversleep, miss his breakfast, get to work late, and that's that."

"But that'll never work," she quickly interrupted. "I've done that lots of times, and he doesn't listen to those threats any more than he listens to others."

"But, Nattie, let me finish. Your method hasn't worked because you've only talked. Now it's time to act."

"Act how?"

"Do not call him a second time."

"But I can't do that, Dr. Hauck. If I do, he'll oversleep, anger his boss, maybe even lose his job," she protested.

"Then I'm afraid you're stuck with the problem. Unless he can *see* that you won't call him again, he'll never believe you. 'Seeing is believing' is the way the old saying goes and it's absolutely true. Try it and see."

This conversation took place before a major holiday weekend during which Gus and his family were planning to go to Chicago. On Saturday morning Nattie got up, told Gus to wake up and get dressed, and then prepared to dress her three children and pack the car. Gus never stirred. She was all set to call him again, but luckily she held her tongue and decided to give my advice an opportunity to work.

Nattie put the children in the car, closed the door behind her, and drove off to Chicago without Gus. When he later woke up and realized what had happened he was furious. But for the first time he could *see* that she meant what she said and that she did what she said. He was absolutely amazed.

They had some hard words Sunday afternoon when she returned, but she calmly told him again she was not responsible for his sleeping habits. She would call him once on weekday mornings and if he wanted to get to work on time, fine. If not, she was willing to move or be temporarily deprived if he had to look for another job.

Gus now had no trouble understanding all this. He was able to *see* she meant business. Talk is cheap, but one act is also worth a thousand words. When Gus *saw* that the family had left him behind, he became an instant believer. It worked like a miracle.

Charlotte achieved instant respect from her father when she stopped complaining to him about his unreasonable requests and simply denied his wishes. She wrote me the following account.

"The bus depot called Dad and informed him he had left his ticket there. Dad said someone would pick it up for him. He called me and asked if I was going to visit Mother that day. I said no. Then he asked if I was going in for any reason. I said no. I finally asked him why, and he told me about his ticket. I told him I would be glad to pick it up for him on Monday. His voice immediately changed from the soft, almost melodic tone he employs when he wants you to do something for him to one of a higher pitch. He said, 'Well, it really should be picked up today, since they have already called me about it.' I replied, 'If that is the case, Dad, maybe you should drive over there today and get it.'

"My refusal to do immediately as he suggested was too much for him, and he started to choke and he coughed for thirty seconds. Then he said I would still be expected to pick it up today.

"The next day he called and asked why I hadn't dropped off the ticket. I told him I had no intention of getting it until Monday.

" 'You mean you didn't pick it up yet?' he asked in amazement.

" 'That's right, Dad. I didn't pick it up yesterday and I won't do it until Monday. Sorry, it's the best I can do. Shall I still get it?'

" 'Oh, all right. If you can't, I guess you can't.'

"And then he hung up."

ANALYZE THE ACCUSATIONS

Are you one of those persons who is easily manipulated by others through accusations? If your mate accuses you of spending too much, do you automatically spend less? If you do, you're permitting someone else to run your life. You're being unassertive and you're not saying or doing what *you* mean.

Throwing accusations at you can actually be a technique for getting you *not* to do the thing you're being accused of. A woman who did not like being left alone over the weekend repeatedly accused her husband of not loving her and of wanting to flirt with ladies at the golf course. If he played golf after such accusations, he thought he would be agreeing with her. So he stayed home to prove how completely mistaken she was. Her trick worked. She really didn't believe he was unloving at all, just interested in a sport that she did not like and that kept him away all day. By using a little guilt and trying to demean him, she easily accomplished what would have been impossible if she had tried to order him to stay home. The husband was a victim of manipulation. He could have exerted polite power on his wife if he had understood the following three courses of action for dealing with accusations.

1. He could have asked himself simply if the accusation was true or false. If true, he could further ask if it was objectionable or acceptable. For example, suppose he agreed with his wife that he was neglecting her by being gone most of every Saturday. And maybe he did like socializing on the course. His first duty to himself is to analyze whether or not he is behaving fairly or unfairly in so doing.

In either event he need not feel guilt and thereby allow himself to be controlled by his wife. If he believes she is too dependent on him and needs to be forced to be more sociable on her own, he could then agree with his wife and say to himself: "Yes, honey, I am neglecting you on Saturdays. But I think you need friends of your own. I know it seems I'm being unloving, but actually I'm doing this for your own good." In this way he could agree partly with her accusations and still not feel guilty or want to change.

2. But suppose he agrees with her. Should he feel guilty then? No, he still doesn't need to feel guilty and can still want to change. He'd be saying something like

the following to himself. "I didn't realize I was neglecting my wife. It never dawned on me she was so lonely. She's right to accuse me of thoughtlessness. No wonder she thinks I don't love her. I'll surely change this next weekend, and I don't think I'm bad just because I was thoughtless. I'm a mistake-making human being. I'm not perfect, and no matter how hard I try I'm always behaving badly to some extent."

3. If he thinks about her accusations deeply, he may decide she is wrong and he'll simply discount her statements. "It's not true that I ignore her. I've asked her along a million times, and she never comes. All she wants to do for fun is play bridge. I'm an active person and must get some exercise. And I don't flirt with the ladies at the course. I'm friendly with them, that's all. If she's jealous, that's her problem and she'll have to learn how to get over that. So I have no intention of staying home on the one day of the week I can play golf when I've given her my company the other six days."

If you'll analyze any accusation and consider these three possibilities, you'll be able to deal with it nicely. For a more complete view, you may want to read my book *Overcoming Frustration and Anger.* Once you learn how to handle accusations, you'll be surprised at how free of domination you will feel.

WHEN TALK IS NOT RECOMMENDED

When two people are not getting along, the first element in their relationship to look for as a source of the difficulty is their communication. Are they each expressing themselves openly and fully? Usually not. Only when their deepest feelings are identified and talked about do the distances between them lessen while understanding increases.

This is only another example of the old advice asking us to sit down and reason together. To do that, the parties involved talk about their views and, it is hoped, calmly arrive at a decision.

But there are times when talk between two persons is a waste of time. There are times when talking to someone is nothing but manipulation, and I advise strongly against engaging in such conversations.

Take the typical case of a man and woman who have been in a dispute for weeks. He wants to deposit more money in the savings account, she wants it in the checking account. They've talked about it numerous times but have not reached an agreement they can live with. Each payday he puts away more money into savings than she approves of and each payday she has another heart-to-heart talk with him, believing he simply doesn't understand her views. Perhaps another go-around will get him to see it her way by removing his confusion or lack of understanding.

But will it? He knows what she'll say. They've been over that ground a dozen times. Still she'll go on believing that he will change his mind if he could only understand her. The obvious reason he doesn't agree with her (according to her) is that he doesn't comprehend her thinking.

Why is it so difficult to realize that we can understand each other and still disagree? For example, there is no lack of understanding between the Western countries and the Communist bloc. They want society one way, we another. There is no way either is going to change the views of the other drastically by sitting down and talking some more.

The same could be said about your sexual preferences. As a heterosexual you prefer being intimate with the opposite sex. Would you seriously suggest that by sitting down and reasoning the thing out I could convert a homosexual to prefer the opposite sex or that the homosexual could persuade me to prefer my own sex?

Changes do occur between sexes and nations but slowly and only when the party is ready for change. Another powwow is not going to bring some magical agreement because a point was made that finally broke the deadlock. I wish that were so.

Accept the fact that once both views have been well expressed, more talk signifies a refusal to agree. That's what the husband felt when his wife insisted they talk again about their money matters. It didn't dawn on her that he could be understanding her very well and yet not think she was right.

So what is she to do? She could convert her talk to action and bring the issue to a head by ordering things she wanted and then see if he'd tolerate that. Or she could put aside money slowly and then buy the furniture. Or she could tolerate the whole thing and let the matter rest because it wasn't all that important. Or she could do other creative things, who knows? Any of them would be better than another argument.

MOCK ANGER

Polite power is expressed by a technique that parents have been using since babies were born. To *pretend* you are angry is an excellent way of making your point and getting your way at the same time.

If you were visiting your friends and had your children along, you could easily encounter this situation: the host offers your child a piece of candy. To be polite you tell your son it's okay to have one piece, but just this one. Fifteen minutes later the lad sneaks up to you and asks for another piece. You politely tell him he can't have any more. But he doesn't let it rest at that. He pesters you with tugging at your clothing, whines, and threatens to throw a tantrum.

All of this is cute up to a point, but before long you tire of it and then you stop all the nonsense very suddenly in the same way every mom and dad has done it in the past. You yell and the child senses the danger he is in and quiets down. He may be back much later, but for the present he has been dealt with.

The important thing to remember about these frequent outbursts, however, is that this is mock anger. You really don't want to kill anyone. Often you even knew that before you supposedly blew your top. The person who uses this mock anger says to himself: "Well, it looks like I'm going to have to settle this problem quickly. I'll *pretend* I'm angry and that will get action out of my children. Later, when we have more time to discuss the problem, I can take time to explain how I really feel."

Mock anger is imperative when a child is near danger and you want to warn him or her to stay on the sidewalk, or not to get too close to the railing. One of the best ways to make your point at such critical moments is to pretend great anger. The child will respect and fear you and that's just what is needed when a child is about to walk out into the street.

In moderation it is a good technique in business or in a marriage. An employee who is working sloppily can get the point rather quickly if you show real irritation with his work. But while you're *acting* mad you can be as cool as a penguin. You realize that he's human, that he has lots to learn, and that a gentle reminder won't impress him enough. So you emphasize it with a mean look and a sharp tone in your voice. Your point is well made and later you can act as though nothing happened.

You had better be careful of how often you use this technique, however. Use it too much and you get those around you to think you're truly angry most of the time. And you can't be sure you won't turn this device into a habit. Mock anger, to be mock anger, has to be used only on rare occasions when gentle persuasion appears to be ineffective. It is one of those tools in everyone's bag of tricks which are best employed if not overdone.

Politeness, good manners, and discussion are still the best ways to talk to others. However, if your television set has been at the repair shop for three weeks when you expected it to be home in one, and if your polite phone calls have not caused things to move along, let me suggest you keep calm inwardly the next time you call the shop but sound mad outwardly. See if that doesn't get some action. Then, when you hang up the phone you'll turn to your mate and ask sweetly, "Another cup of coffee, dear?"

YOU DON'T HAVE TO ANSWER

A friend of mine was in a drugstore when a neighbor came up and began asking personal questions about my friend's daughter. My friend simply did not answer the woman.

You can make the claim that a civil question deserves a civil answer. But the point can also be made that you don't owe explanations about your private life to just anyone who happens to ask about it. Most persons answer such questions because they don't want to appear rude, not appreciating fully the fact that rudeness is sometimes shown by the person doing the asking.

Have you ever been asked how much money you make? Did you answer? If you did, I trust it was only to someone who had a decent right to know, such as a family member or the IRS. If you answered such a personal question to the fellow you met at the party, you had better watch yourself, because you're allowing the poor opinion of others to mean too much to you.

"But how can you simply ignore a person's questions? It would make you look like a positive fool, wouldn't it?" you ask.

No one makes a fool of you, ever has, or ever can. Whether you feel like a fool depends entirely on how you interpret what's going on. My friend, for instance, could have said: "How humiliating this is. I'm not answering her questions. She must take me for a fool."

But she could just as well have told herself (and been more rational besides): "I know she'll think I'm strange, but that's her problem. She has no business prying into my family life and if it takes silence or ignoring her to make my point, so be it. I don't like being this way, but she gives me little alternative. If she rejects me, too bad. It's more important that I do what I think is right, feel good about standing up for myself and endure the rejection, than it is to please her, to go against my principles."

This technique takes a strong personality. Most people don't have the self-confidence to ignore direct questions. However, if you're one of those nice people who were trained always to speak when spoken to, here's your chance to try something new and to grow besides.

KINDS OF ASSERTIVENESS

Not only is it important to be yourself but equally as important is how you do it. There is style involved in putting your foot down as well as putting your best foot forward. For practical purposes I have divided the ways people stand up for themselves into two groups: diplomatic assertion and vulgar assertion.

When you are at a highway café and the waitress brings you cold coffee, you can calmly ask her to please bring you a cup of hot coffee. That would be an example of diplomatic or polite power. If, on the other hand, you call back the waitress and protest so everyone hears you, that's an example of vulgarity. It is the most common form of power used to influence another person. It is also the poorest way to do it.

Most people don't realize how often they resort to vulgar power. Each time a parent with loud voice intimidates a child, vulgar assertion is being used. Why can't Mother or Father merely say what is displeasing, penalize the child for misbehaving, and then stop? Must they humiliate and blame and demean as well? I think not.

You *can* assert yourself with dignity and firmness. You *don't* have to be a dictator or a screaming maniac to make your point. The husband, for example, who is tired of beans and hot dogs for three suppers in a row does not have to throw the food against the wall and scare his children to make his point, as good as it might be. That's vulgar behavior pure and simple.

All of us are guilty of vulgar behavior from time to time because we are raised with the idea that it's mature to be rough to defend our rights. People boast about how loud they are when they roast someone over the coals. They feel weak and passive when they treat others gently but firmly.

Brewster was head of a large company that started losing money a year after he was elevated to his new post. A firm of psychological consultants studied his operation and found that his company was suffering from him. In board meetings he was a brash dictator. Every few weeks he'd take one of his junior executives to task and try to improve his performance by vulgarly pointing out his faults in front of the entire group.

He actually believed he was being effective by humiliating his staff. It was the manly thing to do. Chew out your staff regularly in no uncertain terms, he thought, and you assert your authority and gain respect. Perhaps, but at what price!

As the months rolled by, this bully began to lose his best men. In the end he was left with less creative and less intelligent workers who were willing to tolerate his rudeness. Gradually his company lost ground.

Street gangs, dictators, bullies, and powerful but insecure people have all been known to use this vulgar form of influence. They may get their way, to be sure, but the way they get it creates more problems than it solves.

There are several things that can be said for quiet dignity and polite power. First, it reflects the better side of human nature. Animals snarl at each other. People speak to each other. A mark of civilization is the habit of conversing with our enemies in tones of dignity and respect. Few behaviors are as offensive as raw, uncouth scoldings. The man who takes an item back to the store and acts as if selling a faulty toaster was the greatest crime since the Lindbergh kidnapping isn't acting like a civilized man.

To attempt to humiliate the salesgirl or the store owner before other customers is the height of inconsiderateness. It is unnecessary and it is not in good taste.

Mark Twain, when he toured Europe, was impressed with the way the French police handled traffic. If a pedestrian stepped into the traffic, the policeman would politely wave the person back to the curb or even go up to that person and explain why he did so. By contrast, Twain thought, an American policeman would have blown his whistle, yelled loudly for the pedestrian to get back on the curb, and not spared the citizen's feelings at all. I always thought that was a good example of polite versus vulgar power.

A second advantage of friendly persuasion is its effectiveness. Being considerate about a request usually gets more cooperation than being brusque does. Not always, of course, but often enough. At least it's worth trying first to see what the effect will be. Then, if you don't get satisfaction, you can always become more insistent.

Ever hear of the power struggle? That's a situation

that develops when you try to prove you're more powerful than someone else while that person tries to prove greater power over you. Think of two bull moose, heads down, horns locked, shoving each other back and forth on a hillside.

People are very much the same. Push them and they spitefully push back. Order your children not to smoke and they likely will smoke more. Insist that your mate be on time to pick you up and the opposite may happen.

Most of us do not want to be told what to do. What's even worse is being ordered rather than advised. Either approach is tolerable. But when you order someone nastily, don't expect smiles of gratitude for your efforts. You're going to earn that person's disapproval and possibly outright resistance.

As I see it, if you want to get your way in this world but you don't have the power of a Hitler or a Stalin, assert yourself with dignity. With respect for the other person, with politeness and friendly persuasion, you will get much farther in the long run. Even if you must exert unusual power such as taking someone to court, or firing a lazy clerk, such acts can be performed with all the firmness that is needed while at the same time maintaining dignity for both parties.

THE DANGER OF INDULGING THE LADIES

Many men believe that being *very* nice to women is the best way to guarantee their love and respect. In other words, the more you do for a woman, the more she'll love you.

This appears to be common sense. If you knocked yourself out for me, be you male or female, I know for certain that I'd have a very warm spot in my heart for you. That's only natural.

Not so with many women. Here is where the rule breaks down. Women do not want to be catered to by the important men in their lives. They don't mind your being attentive, tender, and caring, but be careful that you do not do everything they ask or you'll lose them. That's right, lose them.

Before a woman can love you she generally has to respect you. If she loses respect for you, she loses the love too. Therefore, you are wiser usually to stand your ground with your lady friend, deny her from time to time, and assert yourself over her occasionally. She'll respect you for it. Of course the way you say and do what you mean is important. Be decent about your firmness and she can still like you although you're frustrating her.

One of the clearest examples of this behavior can be seen in adolescents. The high school boy takes his girl to a movie. To show his respect for her he asks which movie she wants to see. They go there. Afterward, he again asks her where she'd like to go for a bite to eat. They go there. They meet some of their friends and he wants to accept an invitation to bring his girl to the home where all the gang is going after they finish at the restaurant, but he asks her first. She wants to go home. They go home.

The poor fellow probably thinks he's making a great hit. Little does he realize that by never disagreeing with his girl he gives her the impression he's spineless, that he doesn't have a mind of his own, or that he's so desperate to win her approval he'll put up with almost anything. Try to understand fully what the girl really feels. After he has been a living doll all evening long, she thinks less of him than she did before the evening started.

Women want a man to be strong, not weak. They want to lean upon him and accept direction from him at times, not to run his life or he hers. She's trying to find out just how much he will take before he puts his foot down and his shoulders back. If he were to assert himself kindly but firmly once in a while, she'd have a great deal more respect for him. And after developing respect, she'd feel more loving.

This means that if our young high school student picked up his date and said on occasion, "Tonight we're going to the Main Theater and to Jim's Chinese Restaurant afterward," he'd be scoring more points than he would if he sought to please her all the time.

That's not the full story, however. More often than not the woman will not take being dominated and she'll protest. For all the world it will seem to the man that she is angry and that her love is rapidly fading.

Don't worry. That's true only when you are a constant dictator and when you practically always get your way. But if you want your way once in a while and you honestly feel that you're not being selfish, stick to your guns. Some interesting things will happen.

First, she'll complain of not getting her way. If you've been fair all along, don't listen to this. It is her way of testing you. She wants to see if she can manipulate you, wrap you around her finger. So she makes those noises, hoping down deep that you'll stand up to her and say, "No." If you do, she may protest again outwardly but be relieved inwardly, or she may actually smile and appreciate the manly way you stood by your decision.

The more unsure a woman is of your strength, the more she may test it. Sometimes she'll push you so far that you may have to choose between giving in to her or face a breakup. This may still be that game she's playing. Stand pat when you know you are in the right. If you're strong enough inwardly to stand her rejection, your chances of earning her admiration go up greatly. She then knows that you cannot be manipulated, her threats of leaving you don't scare you, and you must be pretty secure. That impresses her and lets her feel she has a strong man, one she can lean on once in a while.

SWEET JAKE

Betty had a problem with Jake. Anything she wanted from him she got. He didn't know the word "No." Time after time she'd test him, hoping he'd protest, but sweet Jake loved his wife and couldn't stand to see her unhappy. Small wonder it baffled him to see his marriage slipping away, even after he tried so hard to be decent. The nicer he was, the less she felt for him.

At times Betty wondered if she should divorce Jake and take up with an old boyfriend who treated her much more firmly. When I saw what was going on, I told Jake what his wife required and urged him to stop being the completely sweet and giving fellow he had been for the past five years.

He could hardly believe his ears. The thought of getting Betty to love him more by asserting himself zonked him. At first he simply couldn't follow my instructions, but when she asked for a separation he decided to take me seriously. One evening after telling his wife he would attend a professional meeting, she told him that she and her girl friend would go out to a bar for the evening.

His instinctive reaction was to be the nice guy and tell her to have a good time. He caught hold of himself, however, and blurted out in a very firm voice: "No you're not. You're staying here until I get back. If you want to go to a bar, I'll take you to one."

So flabbergasted was she over this firm stance that she didn't have wits enough to protest. Instead, she felt an immediate sense of relief and said no more. When I spoke with her later she appeared calm. She wasn't thinking of another man, and when speaking of her husband's refusal to tolerate her going to a bar, she had a broad, contented smile on her face.

Men, if you want your woman to love you, do not love in return at any price. Draw a line beyond which you will not go, even if the marriage will be sacrificed. That's one of the best ways to preserve the marriage. Women want to rely on the strength in their man. They don't want a chump. And the best proof they have that their man is strong is when he will tolerate some rejection from his wife. If men can tolerate the threat of separation or divorce, then they can obviously tolerate lesser distresses. And that's precisely what the women want to know.

DON'T MAKE IDLE THREATS

The essence of asserting yourself is to say and do what you mean. Back up your words with action. No one can take you seriously if you promise repeatedly to object to your noisy upstairs neighbor for throwing wild parties and then never do it. Even your children won't believe you unless you back up your brave talk occasionally with an actual demonstration.

Personnel managers of large companies report repeated infractions of the rules by employees largely because supervisors don't act upon their threats. I know of one man who was late several times in one month and was called on the carpet for this. He was cautioned that he could get suspended if he didn't shape up.

The next time he was tardy the boss accepted his excuse and simply admonished him not to let it happen again. And it didn't happen again, at least for a while. Then he called in sick because of a hangover. He was a likable chap and the boss didn't want to see the employee lose his job. He gave him a few loud words over the phone and told him to be sure to be at work tomorrow. The boss suspected he had been lied to but didn't make much of it.

You can surely figure out the ending to this story. The time eventually came when all the idle threats by the foreman turned into one sudden act of determination and the young fellow found himself out on the street with his toolbox.

Such handling of irritating problems occurs all too often. It is a waste of time, teaches the offender to goof off, turns the relationship between employer and employee or between parent and child into a struggle, and leaves everyone unhappy in the long run.

A much better way of handling a noncooperative employee is to do what the manager of a large sales firm did to a salesman who had recently been flown in from out of state. He was told on two occasions to straighten out, but he didn't listen well. At that point the manager called him into his office, politely asked him to sit down, and said something like the following.

"Look, John, let's stop fooling ourselves. You're not working out in our organization and I therefore want you to leave. Apparently you don't like the way we operate and I can accept that. However, it's clear to us you'll be happier elsewhere and we offer you our best wishes. Here is your severance pay and a plane ticket home. If you like, I'll be glad to drive you to the airport."

Parents can do the same with a child who has been warned not to whine. Instead of giving another warning, simply take hold of his arm and lead him off to his room. "What? Not give an explanation?"

Right. Don't give an explanation. You've already done that with your previous warnings. If you don't want to make idle threats, you had better back up your talk with action. Preferably action without another explanation. You'd be surprised how effective this technique is.

Do you *really* want to be believed? Do you *truly* want to exercise polite power over those close to you? Then keep quiet for a change and *show* that person the result you promised so often before. That's not always easy to do. But if you don't do it this way, you'll find that making more idle threats is much harder on everyone concerned in the long run.

WHEN THREATS ARE VALID

Pamela was overdrawn on her checking account for the fifth time. Wally had finally had his fill and said, "If you can't keep the records straight, I'm going to take over the checking account."

Her response was quick and typical: "Are you threatening me?"

Isn't that an interesting remark? What difference does it make whether he is threatening her or not? The point is that she had better keep her addition and subtraction straight or he'll do it for her. Call it a threat or call it a promise. The end result is apparently going to be the same.

But people don't see it that way. If they interpret such a remark as a threat, they then have to defy it. That's why they ask in all seriousness, "Are you threatening me?" The unspoken remainder of that thought is: "Because if you are, I have no intention of changing. Neither you nor anyone else is going to tell me how I have to run my checkbook."

Whether it's a threat or a promise depends on how you take it. If you're supersensitive, you'll think you're being attacked and put down. If you're not defensive about it, you'll interpret it as a prediction, nothing else.

Is it a threat if your boss tells you he'll fire you if you come in late just one more time? If you think it is, then tell me, how can he make the same prediction without its being a threat? Must he say it calmly? Is that what changes a threat into a promise? Not according to many people I've spoken to. They interpret every prediction and request for change as a threat. When the boss tells them, "Come in on time or don't come at all" and does this sweetly and with a smile, it can still be viewed as a threat.

Don't bother yourself over this issue at all. The person who talks like this is trying to convey important messages: get here on time or I'll fire you; be kinder to me or I'll leave; don't spend so much money or I'll close the account; etc. These are all strong statements and call for serious consideration. Just because they are serious, there is usually a consequence you can expect if you go against the warning.

When you are asked a favor, there may or may not follow a warning of what will happen if you do not grant the favor. When you take offense at being told what the end result will be if you frustrate your mate or your friend, you hear only the first part of the statement and the second part goes underground. Then, after you've frustrated the person hundreds of times, you may find that person breaking away from you and you'll be shocked and amazed.

However, had you not been so sensitive about being threatened, you would wisely have *welcomed* hearing what would result if you did not go along. If you want to avoid future surprises, *ask* what the person intends to do if you don't go along. Then you can control the situation and make a decision based on all the facts, not half of the facts.

If she says, "Come home to dinner on time," you had better ask, "Or what?" She might say, "I'll eat alone," or "I'll throw your food out," or "I'll not cook again for a week," or "I'll leave you," or any number of other options. Wouldn't you want to know which of those outcomes you'll be facing if you frustrate her again? Frying your own hamburger is a whole lot different from coming home to an empty house.

ASSERTION IN AN EMERGENCY

Are there ever times when a rude or selfish manner is not only tempting but necessary for your health? Yes, there are. At such times taking the bull by the horns has achieved results not likely in any other way. Fortunes have been made by business czars precisely because they broke the rules and did things as they wanted. They were the super self-asserters of the world. They wanted something and worked the world and the people in it to their advantage. If you want to build an empire, establish a shipping company, span a continent with railroads, you can hardly do so by playing the game in the decent way we would like to be treated.

Sometimes, to save your life, you had better put your foot down in a most daring way. Only those who know how to make things happen can achieve this. Take the true case of an inmate of a concentration camp. Just before the Americans came to liberate them, the prisoners were driven from the front lines in the dead of winter. Many died of exposure. Finally they arrived one cold night at a home that could house only a small number of the entire group. All those who were not very warmly clothed were sure to die while waiting outside until dawn.

A doctor in the group reasoned that he would die from the cold if he did not get into the warm building. So, to save his life, he turned con artist and lied his way past the Gestapo guard. He was admitted and soon blended into the inner group, where his life was saved and he could write of the incident years later.

Is such behavior moral? I'm not sure. However, it is clear that you cannot be considerate of others in all cases and survive. No doubt there were others in the company of the concentration camp doctor who wanted to find comfort in the building, but because they let people push them around, they froze to death.

In such instances it is critical that you learn to assert yourself and *make* things happen. When you do, the entire course of your life can change.

Can this behavior be misused and can it take unfair advantage of other people's decencies? I think so. Here is what happened in World War II. The city is Liège, Belgium.

I drove the lieutenant, a language professor, into town and after a fine lunch of chicken and wine he suggested we take a bath. A line of soldiers stretched from the second floor of the bath all the way down to the street. Without blinking an eye he gave me instructions to follow him. So we walked by the whole line as though we owned the place, stepped out in front of the soldier who was next for a bathtub stall, and went down the row of stalls trying each door until we each found a vacant tub. We locked ourselves in our stalls and drew our baths.

When the lady came around protesting in French that we were out of turn and should leave (I think that's what she said), I simply said something polite in English and pushed the money to her under the door.

She picked up the money and left us alone. After a comfortable and much-needed bath (the first in three months for me), we dressed, left the building and went past the same line of men who were still waiting patiently, got into our jeep, and headed for the front lines.

I've always had good and bad feelings about that incident—good that I finally washed myself, bad that I took advantage of others and did something I would not have enjoyed if it had been done to me. But it does demonstrate how things can be done in unorthodox ways if you have courage.

6

Melinda Grows Up

FIRST SESSION

Melinda started out the first session by telling me how dominated she had been by her parents through their anger and guilt. Like several other women I have counseled, she too was having trouble marrying the man of her choice against the strong protests of her parents.

CLIENT: My folks met John, but he didn't make a very good impression. They insisted I could do much better, that he was hardly what they expected.

I told them I'd marry him anyway, but they said, "Absolutely not."

My mother would cry and lie in bed for days. However, we became engaged two years ago, but I haven't been able to go through with the wedding because I am afraid of how they will react.

THERAPIST: You haven't had the courage to marry him for the past two years?

C: Right. I finally set a date for last Saturday but backed out again, for the third time.

T: You were going to marry this fellow this past Saturday?

150

C: Yes.

T: And you called it off because your parents would object to it?

C: Yes, because I hadn't told them. I didn't know how to tell them and I knew that telling them would cause the biggest rift between us. At that point I realized there was a problem I haven't been able to solve.

T: What is it?

C: I'd feel guilty.

T: You're afraid to stand up to your folks? Now why is that?

C: You're not supposed to.

T: Who says so?

C: My folks.

T: Does that make them right?

C: No. It's just that I can't take seeing my mother go into hysteria.

T: Why? Because you believe that you make her hysterical?

C: I know I don't. I can sit back right now and convince myself I can't possibly make her hysterical, she does it to herself. But once I get into that situation I lose all track of that kind of reasoning.

T: In other words you say: "I did this. I am really upsetting my mother. Look what a bad daughter I am." Is that it?

C: Yes.

T: Okay. The other thing you're thinking is that you don't dare upset your parents because they will reject you and you couldn't possibly stand that.

C: Right.

T: Okay. How old are you now?

C: I am twenty-seven.

T: Twenty-seven? Now do you really, really still need your mother and father's undying love, their approval?

C: No, I don't. I have been supporting myself for five years, and I find that when I don't have any contact with them I do fine. But when I'm with them, all of a sudden I feel like I am three years old again. I resent it and I am extremely angry.

T: You have never told them that?

C: I never told them just how really angry I have been for the past several years, because I would sooner back off and go my own way instead of having this out with them.

T: Do you really want to make a change? Are you prepared to face the music and just have them reject you?

C: Yes, because I am getting to the point where I personally am not happy with it anymore. I am not happy when I make a decision based on my parents' view. The part that makes me most angry is that I worry so much about what they think and how they feel.

T: That's not you. The question is, How did you get into that condition? First, you are *letting* people make you feel guilty. They can't do that without your cooperation. And secondly, you are saying: "If I don't agree with them and do everything they say, they will reject me and *I couldn't stand it if my mother and father didn't love me. They must love me at all times. I can't possibly live with their rejection.*" Nonsense. They don't make you feel guilty. You have a right to your own desires, and if they get upset, that is *their* problem. If they reject you, that's too bad.

That mattered when you were three years old, but it hardly matters at twenty-seven. It does matter, of course, but not *that much* when you have to deny yourself the choice of a husband. Or to be married at all. Or to make a trip. Or whatever. Come on, when are you going to grow up? What is it going to take? How old do you have to be before you start saying: "Okay, Mother and Father, you want to reject me. Go ahead." Do you really need their approval anymore?

C: No. But that's the whole thing. I know I don't need their approval but—

T: But what?

C: But when I get back into the situation I just cringe.

T: Because? What are you saying to yourself at that point that makes you cringe?

C: I don't know.

T: They're going to get terribly upset and I'm going to feel responsible. You are *still* saying that. You know that's not true, but you don't believe that at the moment of truth.

The other thing you don't believe is that rejection doesn't hurt. At the moment you stand up for yourself you think: "But it does hurt. I can't possibly think of alienating myself from these people and never have them talk to me again. It would be unbearable." I think not. First of all, they *are* going to come around. Most parents come around. They may protest, they may not like their son-in-law, but they *will* come around especially when there are grandchildren.

In any event, you are no longer a child. At the moment you stand up to them, remember that. Okay?

C: Okay.

SECOND SESSION

In the second session we see that Melinda has a strong reaction to my remarks. Sensing that I was trying to be helpful without worrying about her rejecting me, she tried some assertion of her own. She has decided to marry her fiancé against the wishes of her folks. She also stands up to him (after one session in therapy) and sets a date that suits *her*.

C: I was so mad at you. I had talked to the minister and he was consoling. I enjoyed that, because that's what I'm used to when I'm upset. You weren't that way at all. It's just like you looked at me and said: "Here are the facts. When are you going to grow up? You don't have to be that way." I never had anyone sit back and be so direct. Either you are going to do it or you're not. And that made me angry. But that's good, because it's the first time I ever really faced it.

T: Did you have the feeling you wanted to walk out?

C: About fifteen minutes after I sat down I just wanted to walk out. He doesn't care about my feelings was my first reaction.

T: I'm glad you didn't leave. You talked to your fiancé?

C: He picked me up and I got in the car and slammed the door. And he said, "Well, how did it go?" And I said: "I hate the man. I'm never going back." He said, "How come?" And I said: "You know what he said? He asked me when I was going to grow up." That's when he turned to me and said that it was the truth. "The reason you hate him is that you can't fight the truth." Going home that day, I began to realize that I had really been shortchanged. As far as my folks go,

I have compromised feelings. I have compromised values, and they haven't done it to me. They are living happily and I'm in misery and that doesn't quite seem fair. I also thought about when you said, "If people really love you, they are not going to use guilt to make you miserable." I thought that made sense. If they truly care in the way they say they do, they are going to watch out for my feelings too. It's not going to be a one-way street. If you care for a person, you are not going to manipulate her by her feelings, because that's just not right. All those things are beginning to fall into place.

T: Fantastic. Well, are we friends again?

C: Yes, I think so.

T: When are you going to get married?

C: I have a contract until July. So I told my fiancé I want to go ahead and stay with this company until then and I set the date for September.

T: And you are ready to go through with it this time?

C: I am ready to go through with it. Yes.

T: You don't think there is going to be any problem with that?

C: I really don't think so. At the end of the year I will be ready for it.

T: Are you putting it off again now by saying next September?

C: No.

T: Why not? What is different about putting if off this time?

C: I understand it now. I think that is what is different about it. I understand what has happened before and I know exactly what I want to get done this year. Before, I was putting it off so I wouldn't have to think

about the problem and confront my parents. I could
say to my fiancé, "Well, you don't have a regular job
yet," and that way I could push this whole problem
about my folks into a corner so I didn't have to think
about it. I think this year is different. I am doing
something about it myself and when I talked to my
fiancé I told him I wanted to go ahead and stay with
my company for my own betterment. And for the
first time I feel like I am doing something to help
myself.

T: So this time you are putting it off for a totally different reason. It is not to please your folks but to please
yourself?

C: Yes. That I am sure about.

THIRD SESSION

In the third of four sessions we begin to see great
progress in Melinda's self-assertion and self-confidence.
She is beginning to think for herself without feeling
guilty.

C: Something happened since the last time I saw you
—a newfound freedom. My mother came into my
house and told me that I should clear out the boxes.
I said: "Mom, I live here. I don't have to do it."

T: You said that?

C: Yes, and she didn't say anything back to me. She was
nice for the whole night. What had happened was she
came in earlier and said, "What are all those boxes
doing there piled up in the corner of your bedroom?"
I said, "I haven't moved them." Then she said, "Well,
I think you ought to." And I said: "I don't have to
move them. This is my place. You want to pay my

rent? You want to pay my bills? Then I'll move the boxes." My mother just looked at me and mumbled under her breath. For the rest of the night she was just fine.

Then Dad called on Sunday evening and said something about having called that afternoon and I wasn't home, and I said, "What do you want?" And he said, "Well, I just called to remind you about such and such." I said, "Dad, that's fine," and he said, "Well, where were you?" I said, "Dad, you don't need to know where I was." I always get shocked when he just backs down. He doesn't say anything. He just kind of looks at me and walks away shaking his head. And the most he will say is, "I just don't know what I'm going to do with you." And he walks away and the whole subject is dropped.

Let me change the subject a bit. It seems trivial but there is this woman at the office I had a run-in with at the end of the year. We used to be very close friends. Last week there was constant backbiting and things of this sort and I was so proud of myself. I went home and I thought: "It doesn't bother me. I didn't get upset. I didn't go home and worry like I usually do."

T: What are you doing with respect to this fellow worker?

C: This past Friday we happened to be in the same room together alone. And I simply turned to her and said, "Okay, Mary, whatever animosity you have is mainly on your part." I just looked at her and said: "I don't really care what you think of me and I don't care what you say about me. Just don't let it come back to me, because I do not appreciate people being that rude and immature about a relationship." That's all I said to her. If anyone asks me about the situation, I will say it is something personal and I would prefer to leave it that way.

T: Is this behavior new to you?

C: Extremely new. Usually whenever a person would get upset with me, even if I believed I was in the right, I would go back and apologize to the person and say, "Please talk about what I did wrong." I was compromising all the time. Or I would sit back and worry about it. If someone said something about me, I would go home and I would just be worried sick. I thought: "What if she goes around telling all these people bad things about me that are not true? They are going to think it's true."

When I knew this whole situation would come up I took a very good look at her and I took a look at myself and I thought: "Okay, fine. She is showing a certain amount of jealousy toward me and I think that is her problem. That is not mine. And anything she has said to people, Well, okay, they know who I am. If they want to pass judgment that is not rightfully founded, that again is their problem. It might hurt me, but it won't kill me."

T: Beautiful, beautiful.

C: That made me feel pretty good.

T: Did you notice how sensibly you are thinking?

C: Yes. It's starting. It really is. It just really is. In the first session you said to me, "It is not a catastrophe." Anytime I start to get upset, I think, "Thirty thousand feet in the air and crashing is a catastrophe." I keep telling myself that over again and all of a sudden I look back on the things that would normally make me nervous and when they start I think, "This is really stupid." I think of all the things that could really have happened to me. I could be starving to death without a job. Or I could be pregnant and without a husband. It kind of helps put things back into perspective.

T: That's beautiful.

C: I'll admit, though, it's hard.

T: But you notice that some of those things you are saying—for example, "It's her problem, not mine"— give you immediate relief. Secondly, "I am not upsetting her. She is upsetting herself. I don't have to feel guilty if I have a heart-to-heart talk with her, or that I am going to hurt her feelings. Because I can't." Were you aware of that?

C: I didn't really think of that. No. I had thought of the idea that she is upsetting herself and I wasn't. I just walked into a room and she became extremely nervous. I just stood there and I thought: "All I have done is walk into a room. The problem is inside her, not me."

T: Right.

C: Yes. That's it. Some days it is hard. It really is. It would be very easy just to fall back and say, "I am so depressed, I am so this and so that." But I force myself. When I get up I just say: "It is not that bad. You are a qualified, talented woman. You are going to deal with these things."

T: Beautiful.

FOURTH SESSION

Melinda had a fourth and final session and it was essentially a repeat of the third. She was on her way to becoming a guilt-free and mature woman who continued to respect others but who had a newfound respect for herself.

She said she'd make another appointment if she needed it. She never called again.

Summary

To lose control of your life is like slow death. Not to be all you could be is one of the greatest regrets a person can experience. All of this comes about because we will not take charge of our own lives. We refuse to lead authentic lives, we don't become what we can become, we don't see life as a short experience that is meant to give us pleasure while at the same time not causing other people unnecessary grief.

I wish all of you a stout heart as you venture forth on this road to self-assertion. You have a right to more than you thought. You do not upset other people in the process of asserting yourself, they do it. Not to do so, not to be strong and assertive when your important desires and needs are called upon, leads to a wasted life, physical and emotional slavery, and serious physical or emotional problems.

Throw your chest out, square your shoulders, stick out your chin, and smile. You are about to let the world know what is important to you.

As I was putting the finishing touches to this page, Kaye called.

"Guess what, Paul."

"You stopped accepting free speaking engagements."

"Right," she laughed with delight. "I never thought I could do it. After you gave me that pep talk at the party I've tried three times to ask for a fee to speak, but I backed down each time. Today, just a short while ago, I finally faced the moment of truth and blurted out the fact that I would have to be paid."

"How did it feel, Kaye?" I asked.

"It was agonizing. Sheer anguish. The woman knew I didn't need the money and that made it all the more difficult. I was afraid she would think I was being mercenary. But, as you said, spit it out, don't delay. Face your fear and you'll feel like a million once you get over the initial strain."

"That's how you feel now?"

"I'm on cloud nine, thank you."

"Say, Kaye, I'm writing a book on self-assertion. Do you mind if I use this example in my summary?"

"Not at all, Paul, if you'll give me an autographed copy."

I was about to assure her I'd be delighted. Instead, I jokingly tested her progress. "Kaye, what if I don't give you a book."

"Then I won't permit you to use the example," she laughed.

She learned. She didn't mean that (I hope), but she was learning how to get what she wanted.

Come to think of it, I wonder if I should assert myself and send her a bill.